THE NEXT LEVEL

Breakthrough Performance Anchored By Faith

MICHELLE GETHERS-CLARK

WESTBOW
PRESS
A DIVISION OF THOMAS NELSON

WestBow Press books may be ordered through booksellers or by contacting:
WestBow Press
A Division of Thomas Nelson
1663 Liberty Drive
Bloomington, IN 47403
www.westbowpress.com
1-(866) 928-1240

ISBN: 978-1-4497-5638-3 (sc)
ISBN: 978-1-4497-5639-0 (hbk)
ISBN: 978-1-4497-5637-6 (e)
Library of Congress Control Number: 2012910605

Printed in the United States of America
WestBow Press rev. date: 07/12/2012

To:
My Husband Rudy, My Late Mother Lee, My Son Gregory,
My Daughter Sophia, and Aunt Vie for your
love and encouragement.

CONTENTS

Section I. Character Attributes

Chapter 1:   Faith 5
Chapter 2:   Authenticity 8
Chapter 3:   Integrity 12
Chapter 4:   Patience 15
Chapter 5:   Compassion 18
Chapter 6:   Accountability 21
Chapter 7:   Humility 25
Chapter 8:   Passion 28
Chapter 9:   Ambition 31
Chapter 10: Wisdom 34
Chapter 11: Competitiveness 37
Chapter 12: Perseverance 40
Chapter 13: Generosity 43
Chapter 14: Grace 46
Chapter 15: Transparency 48
Chapter 16: Consistency 51
Chapter 17: Discipline 54
Chapter 18: Approachability 57
Chapter 19: Strength 60
Chapter 20: Curiosity 62
Chapter 21: Courage 65
Chapter 22: Optimism 68
Chapter 23: Presence 70
Chapter 24: Servant 73
Chapter 25: Personal Brand 77

Section II. Performance Tactics

Chapter 26:   Be Excellent...87
Chapter 27:   Market Your Story 90
Chapter 28:   Create A Plan 94
Chapter 29:   Think..97
Chapter 30:   Focus on the Goal...100
Chapter 31:   Communicate 103
Chapter 32:   Ask for Help...110
Chapter 33:   Increase Knowledge 113
Chapter 34:   Do More 116
Chapter 35:   Resolve Conflict..119
Chapter 36:   Gather Data...122
Chapter 37:   Collaborate...125
Chapter 38:   Follow Protocol...128
Chapter 39:   Make A Decision..131
Chapter 40:   Take Risks..135
Chapter 41:   Lead and Follow 138
Chapter 42:   Give Back...140
Chapter 43:   Improve The Culture 143
Chapter 44:   Prioritize 146
Chapter 45:   Manage Relationships..149
Chapter 46:   Influence 152
Chapter 47:   Transform..155
Chapter 48:   Inspire 158
Chapter 49:   Leadership..161
Chapter 50:   Connect the Dots...165

FOREWORD

Written by Rosa Sabater, Senior Executive, Friend and Mom

The Next Level is for our times.

It is relatively easy to be our best selves at work when we have the wind at our backs. It is another thing entirely to stay true to our moral compass when the environment is toxic—layoffs, record unemployment, salary reductions, unhealthy competition, finger pointing (or maybe just a bad boss). Today, more than at any other time in our recent history, work is hard. It is hard to find work, it is hard to do work, and it is hard to keep work. As we bend into the economic headwinds, we can become frustrated, angry and impatient. Our performance suffers. We lose sight of ourselves.

I was with Michelle Gethers-Clark at an executive off-site meeting in the fall of 2008, the week Lehman went under and the Federal government had to bail out AIG. We all knew something had gone very wrong when all our phones started ringing at the same time calling us into emergency meetings. Because Michelle ran collections at the time, she was in particular demand. Her job: figuring out how to collect money from people who no longer had any. She was on a very hot seat. And she had to sit on it for a year. Yet, I never saw her lose her equanimity or composure. Instead, in the face of tremendous adversity, she became an even better Michelle. She went to the next level.

Two years later Michelle and I found ourselves together for a weekend. As we sat cross-legged on the floor of a hotel room, late at night, I asked her about that time. "How were you able to keep it together when everyone else was losing it around you?" Her response was surprisingly simple: "I have a nobler purpose." Michelle wanted career progression and recognition and compensation and acknowledgement just like we all do. But those weren't her end goals. She was going for something much bigger: personally, her purpose was to live her whole life—inside and outside of work and—as Jesus would want her to.

With scripture as the ultimate guide, Michelle distills 25 years of life and work experience into real wisdom in *The Next Level*. Most business books start with performance enhancers: time management, communication, presentation skills, and negotiation. In *The Next Level*, it is purpose, character, and performance—in that order. What is so special about *The Next Level* is that it tackles the big stuff, but still manages to be practical, action-oriented and easy to digest. Read it cover to cover, or spend time reflecting on one character attribute—either way there is something special to learn here.

PREFACE

The Next Level walks through the door to elevate performance in the workplace, community, and even in your home. Do you have a book or resource that gives you practical advice to improve how you think and behave or improve how you handle issues as they arise? The idea for my writing is an outgrowth of my own need to get guidance to solve workplace issues and having few places to turn for answers. Some of my work days were hard and painful, especially in the first 10 years of my professional career. The actual work was not the challenge. The challenge was me being out of sync with other people and the unwritten process which made it hard to get the job done. I wanted a balanced approach to my professional persona—smart, respectful, results-oriented, and spiritual. There was no central place to get training or answers to address my dynamic needs. The gamut of tools offered by my boss, human resources, colleagues, friends, family, a book, and standard professional development courses only addressed a part of my total need. I often found two places that seemed to address the heart of the matter with useable advice—Bible scriptures and prayer. How could I combine traditional training with lessons from the Bible?

The Next Level represents the 50 key things I pay attention to in business, in the community, and at home. The 50 do not come into play every day but they are often present over a 30-day period. The 50 are grounded in the word of God and have become individual chapters categorized into character attributes and performance tactics for breakthrough success. The blessings I have received as a result of improved character and successful performance over my 29-year professional career are extraordinary and the reason I am inspired to share. Becoming a senior vice president at the American

Express Company and being appointed to several boards of directors was highly influenced by my character and performance.

The Next Level weaves together education, observations, process and procedures, successful conclusions, bad outcomes, workplace interactions, training courses, Bible study, and prayer. Each chapter is a standalone tool. When the chapters are collectively considered inside of a career, it provides a road map to address a variety of workplace and career questions or problems. After all, there are no new problems, just new people experiencing a familiar problem. Like it did for me, I expect *The Next Level* will widen your viewpoint of yourself by no longer limiting your identity to physical appearance, the company name, or job title. With an increased view of yourself, you might start to pursue dreams and aspirations to achieve a new level of success. Your internal motivation could be enhanced. What you value could get refreshed. I am certain the road map will cause you to evaluate how your performance is measured and what you can do better. There is no argument that education, talent, gifts, luck, and a reference can get you part of the way toward obtaining a job, a promotion, a date, and even a seat on a board of directors. However, it is character linked to successful performance that will solidify you at the next level and create lasting value.

The Next Level is for people who want to do more by driving positive results and meaningful impact in companies and in communities. The opportunity to do more is documented in a Hierarchy of Performance, which outlines foundational behaviors, fundamental performance, accelerated performance, and breakthrough contributions. I have had the pleasure of working and sharing my perspective in the United States, Canada, India, and the Philippines. Over the last 15 years, the 50 chapters have become the subject of my speaking engagements, coaching and mentoring sessions, classroom instruction, and motherhood. These discussions have been formal and informal, on stage, in ballrooms, conference rooms, atriums, gardens, kitchen tables, restaurants, offices, cubicles, churches, public transportation, and on conference calls. *The Next Level* invites you to think about life and the workplace through a new lens of faith, character, and action. The 50 succinct chapters are structured with biblical scriptures, workplace expectations, examples of life and career success, advice to elevate performance, and a call to action.

The Next Level as a resource to learn from, ponder, and apply. I know you will experience a breakthrough in your thinking, contribution, and performance as a result of reading one or more chapters.

HOW TO USE: *THE NEXT LEVEL*

To maximize the benefit of reading *The Next Level*, identify your status below (A to E) and use the recommendations. In all cases, consider carving out 49 days to study The Next Level, one hour per day. Conclude on day 50 with chapter 50 to document your thoughts.

A: New to career (1 year or less work experience):
Scan the first section in its entirety. Know what's there, because you will want to come back to it as you start your career and or encounter challenges in the workplace. In the second section, focus on the 'Fundamentals.' You have to get really good at these early on. And, by all means, if your employer offers any professional development in these areas, don't hesitate to participate.

B: In transition between careers or positions:
Change affords a wonderful opportunity to reflect and grow. Take your time with the first section, reading one character trait per day. For example, after you read "Compassion," breathe slowly, and think about how you have (and have not) manifested compassion in the workplace. What are the triggers that give rise to your best and worst self? What can you do to take your demonstrated character and performance to *The Next Level*?

C: Middle manager and mature professional:
At varying intervals, professionals assess their careers and personal aspirations. Read the first section to identify your strengths and opportunities to be your best self. Examine the Hierarchy of Performance to ensure fundamentals and accelerators are part of your existing contribution. Position yourself for breakthrough performance. Are you seeking opportunities to contribute at *The Next Level*?

D: Seasoned and senior professional or leader:

It is hard to be senior in any organization because very few people are willing to tell you when you are misbehaving. You have to catch and correct yourself. At least once a year, read through the character section and the breakthrough performance tactics. Are you manifesting your best self in the workplace? If you are not, you owe it to yourself and the tens, hundreds, or thousands of people who work for you to take your performance to *The Next Level*.

E: Life Assessment:

This is an opportunity to gain insight into yourself, if you want to be a better person in your career, community, and relationships with family and friends. *The Next Level* refers to the workplace which is the accumulation of people, personalities, and skill sets with common goals much like our homes and communities. Take the time to read the first section for life wisdom and leverage section two to achieve your greater purpose. Do you want to be better prepared for the various scenarios of your life?

Bible scriptures referenced in *The Next Level* are *italicized* and extracted from the following translations:

New International Version (NIV)
King James Version (KJV)
The Message (The Message)
New Century Version (NCV)

SECTION I

Twenty five character attributes are supported by 70 biblical scriptures. The presented character traits are not an exhaustive list of things you should and should not be. The information is exposure to some of the personal qualities that will create positive downstream impacts on your life, career, business, and community.

Section I goals:

1. Link character to the word of God.
2. Present the case for how strong character benefits the workplace.
3. Offer advice and examples of character.
4. Enhance how you show up.

*So don't lose a minute in building on what you've been given, complementing your basic faith with good **character** [emphasis added], spiritual understanding, alert discipline, passionate patience, reverent wonder, warm friendliness, and generous love, each dimension fitting into and developing the others.*

– 2 Peter 1:5-9 (The Message)

"People follow character not titles."

1 Faith

The Bible defines faith as *confidence in what we hope for and assurance about what we do not see.* –Hebrews 11:1 (NIV). God provides a visual, intellectual and emotional picture of faith to his disciples when he says *faith can move a mountain from here to there.* –Matthew 17:20 (NIV). *The Next Level: Breakthrough Performance Anchored By Faith* unfolds a story of faith as the foundation for building career success beyond the traditional expectations of financial gratification and power. Faith brings hope and challenges us to believe in something greater than ourselves.

Achieving career goals and moving a business to the next level can be the outcome of faith. When evidence may point to a negative conclusion, faith will surface in the belief of a positive outcome. It only takes a small amount of faith to win in life and in business. God rewards people based on faith and obedience to His word.

Faith is something you can carry for yourself as well as for others. Having faith, working with someone who has faith, and having faith in each other are powerful combinations. We cannot always pick our boss or colleagues, but we can exhibit qualities of faith which are mutually beneficial. For example, faithful can mean maintaining a strong work ethic and encouraging others to do the same when your company announces a planned lay-off.

When adversity and negativity are mounting on the journey to career success, faith can seem futile and prayers unanswered. Do we need faith, a miracle, or both to achieve our aspirations? Be assured that God creates a miracle every day for the faithful. Hope alone is not a strategy. However, God makes a new reality for people who have hope and faith as a core aspect of their character. *Jesus looked at them and said, "With man this is impossible, but with God all things are possible."* –Matthew 19:26 (NIV). During insurmountable situations, faith is a call to action. While faith does not guarantee a specific conclusion, it provides strength to handle disappointment, and humility to handle success. A difficult working relationship with your boss is leading you to pray for a new job so you can quit. Suddenly, your boss announces he is leaving the company. A friend randomly refers you as a candidate for a vice president level interview. The next month your current employer announces they are going out of business, and you immediately land a new job making more money. You have a demanding job with two children when your husband gets diagnosed with cancer—you need to do it all: work, nurture children, and support cancer treatments. *Be on your guard; stand firm in the faith; be courageous; be strong.* –1 Corinthians 16:13 (NIV). Faith can be a partnership that frees you from carrying the concern, issue, or burden alone. We gain freedom by—turning it over to God, putting it in God's hands, or being an instrument for God to use.

One of my faith walks led to my dream job. I wanted to become a senior vice president at American Express. I set it as a goal when I was a manager in 1993. I put my head down and forged ahead through faith, respect, hard work, and results. Self-doubt led me to keep my aspirations quiet. I did not go to the finest schools, I grew up in public housing, I did not have an MBA, and I did not have a corporate role model to guide me in my career. However, my mother and aunt prayed for my prosperity. Education was my way out, and I believed that God's will prevails. Overcoming doubt is an ongoing battle but

I have gained confidence out of moments of triumph (projects with extraordinary results), not dwelling on the few disappointments (bad decisions and unfair treatment), and accepting that my background is an asset. I finally told one person of my desire to be a SVP and he was very supportive. It took 10 years to achieve the goal of the corner office. In 2003, I became a senior vice president because of God's will, my faith, sponsorship from leaders, and a track record of excellent performance. *If you do not stand firm in your faith, you will not stand at all.* –Isaiah 7:9 (NIV). Do you have God and the right people on your team to increase your faith and support your dreams?

Believe the probability of success is greater than the logic of failure.

• • •

2 Authenticity

Brothers and sisters, whatever is true, whatever is noble, whatever is right, whatever is pure, whatever is lovely, whatever is admirable—if anything is excellent or praiseworthy—think about such things. Whatever you have learned or received or heard from me, or seen in me—put it into practice. And the God of peace will be with you. –Philippians 4:8-9 (NIV). God expects us to practice specific and admirable character traits and behaviors.

Authenticity in the workplace is the opportunity to be differentiated from the pack. Authenticity begins with personal attributes defined as: genuine, pure, real, valid, reliable, dependable, and faithful. Is it possible to be all these things in a given day, week, month, year, or lifetime? The answer is yes! The alternative to being authentic is to be counterfeit—not true to one's self, inconsistent, unknown, fake, phony, and bogus.

Ranking authentic as the standard for your behavior makes it easier for employees, customers, and others to interact with you and each other. Authenticity places a high priority on respect for others, personal peace, and doing the right thing even when it is unpopular. The results: respect, peace, and opportunity are the rewards for a career grounded in being genuine.

I define authentic as "being comfortable in your own skin." Authentic people don't always have the right answers, and they are not perfect. Authenticity is a combination of reliable words and actions stated and exemplified. The magical moment of authenticity is the alignment of who you are, what you say, and what you do. The ability to show up and be prepared for any given day or situation tells people you are reliable.

Authentic people balance their approach to solving problems and have a trustworthy disposition. Extreme reactions, behaviors, or attitudes contradict authenticity. For example, while showing emotion can be authentic; crying during every presentation could translate into lack of composure. Joking, laughing, and engaging in side-bar conversations could be viewed as immature or distracting. Additionally, tell-it-like-I-see-it professionals—who do not think before they speak could be perceived as abrasive.

Authenticity is more substantial than a title or being articulate. Instead, authenticity blends human qualities and appropriateness to bring about a connection tied to personal experiences. People find others authentic because the connection is personal through direct interactions or impressions from a distance. Dependability and consistency are some traits of being authentic. What might people say about an authentic experience with someone?—My leader said he would fight to get the needed resources for a project, and he did.—My colleague committed to help assemble a presentation but canceled the day before because her boss needed help with a report. She called as soon as she realized the conflict, which gave me time to create a new plan.—My leader always greets me by name.

What are people saying about you?

An appreciation for the authentic can develop out of experience with the counterfeit. People often validate the authenticity of others. Is your authenticity being validated? Everyone has a different lens for interpreting authenticity. Therefore, you must make authenticity a personal standard—be natural and rely on your personality and knowledge. Every person you interact with will draw a different conclusion regarding whether you are authentic. To your benefit, many people will validate you as authentic when actions and words are sincere, transparent, and accurate. Realize some validations are intellectual connections while others are based on emotional connections. Do people feel a connection to you? Is the connection an outgrowth of working on and solving a complex problem together? Is the connection as simple as sharing the same hobby?

I am authentic because I set parameters for how I operate and I abide by them. I allow people to get to know me personally (my family and values) and professionally (my work style and aspirations). My personal qualities are Christian-based values, structure, humility, friendliness, curiosity, consistency, integrity, transparency, compassion, and ambition. I am who I am, and I bring my qualities to every meeting and occasion. Do you have a set of characteristics that describe what can be expected from you? Authenticity contributes to my success as a corporate leader and effectiveness as a member of the board of directors for organizations in the community. Authenticity earns the trust of others, asks questions, drives results, delivers tough messages, and celebrates victories. Authenticity allows you to get angry, laugh, cry, and when it is the right thing to do; to apologize.

The confidence to be authentic is a process. The process can prompt a decision to change behaviors as you witness your own insincerity. Early in my career, I wanted to make positive impressions by wearing high-end clothing and being associated with a specific crowd. I was a junior accountant spending too much money on clothes and basing relationships on status. That approach to life and career ended because I was always broke with superficial friendships. Life was all about me and the external façade. God intervened and spoke to my heart. I shifted gears and found my spirituality again. I began volunteering at church and in the community, and became more grateful for my career successes. Today I remain informed by my past. I enjoy being my authentic self. In the workplace, authenticity resulted in asking one of my bosses to exclude me from discussions that included disparaging, sarcastic, and cynical remarks about others. These useless discussions were becoming commonplace and interfered with working relationships. The comments were mean spirited such as "That man is a waste, he has no idea what is going on." One day I had heard enough and got the courage to ask to be excluded. My boss was surprised by my request but knew his behavior was inappropriate. He stopped being negative about others in front of me.

What makes you authentic? What behaviors do you exhibit to create a sense of peace for you and others?

Being vulnerable allows you to be authentic.

• • •

3 Integrity

The integrity of the upright guides them but the unfaithful are destroyed by their duplicity. –Proverbs 11:3 (NIV). Integrity is a pillar for success while dishonesty leads to destruction.

Integrity imbedded in the employees and the business model of an organization is a critical success factor. Integrity links moral character and ethical behavior. The formal definition of integrity is the adherence to moral and ethical principles; soundness of moral character; honesty. Integrity is also viewed as sincerity and principle.

Integrity said another way, is doing the right thing, expecting the right thing to be done by others, and expecting policies, procedures, and systems to be accurate. These expectations seem simple and doable like not stealing paper, pens, and pencils from the office. So why do these very basic rules become a problem in a career?

There is a daily compromise of integrity to gain power, knowledge, and money. Families, companies, and even churches collapse when the moral code of conduct is abandoned. While competitiveness is a natural instinct, using dishonesty to win is always wrong. The desire to know more, have more, and influence more can cause poor judgment.

Similarly, matters that seem ambiguous can cause a lapse of integrity, leading an otherwise honest person to do something wrong for the sake of keeping a job or avoiding a commotion.

A paycheck, a bigger paycheck, a bonus, and a bigger bonus are temptations for any person. What you will do to get them is a matter of integrity. *A thick bankroll is no help when life falls apart, but a principled life can stand up to the worst.* –Proverbs 11:5 (The Message)

Standards for integrity exist at every juncture in life—God provides the 10 commandments, parents train children on the difference between right and wrong, character development lessons are taught in schools, colleges mandate ethics classes in most fields of study, companies write code of conduct manuals, and professional organizations offer ethics as continuing professional education. Still, many give up their integrity and many more are tempted to be dishonest. Society has a get-ahead-by-any-means-necessary attitude. Worse, reporting an incident of a lapse in integrity is often ignored and ostracized.

I worked as an accountant and internal auditor for a small service company. I was documenting workflows and observed that manual and automated checks were written by one person. This was within the job scope. The bank statement and canceled checks were also handled and reconciled by this person. This was a segregation of duties problem. The organization was at risk for errors not being detected or fraud. I brought this to the attention of the controller. Several rationalized excuses surfaced–the staff size was small and the confidential nature of check payees required limited people in the process, people running the process were trustworthy, and company leaders were looking over shoulders to double check transactions. However, there were no controls, and it was not the right process for any company. No changes were made to the process. I resigned to work in an environment more committed to control and compliance. Unfortunately, some years later it was discovered that the controller embezzled a significant amount of money. A lack of integrity in the process (check writing and bank statement reconciliation) allowed this embezzlement to happen.

The way to eradicate the lack of integrity that exists in schools, businesses, communities, and government, is to hold ourselves to high moral standards through personal codes of conduct. The will to do the right thing is not written in a policy manual or discussed in a lecture. Doing the right thing is an internal value system that guides thinking and behavior. Do the right thing when nobody is looking. *In everything set them an example by doing what is good. In your teaching show integrity and seriousness and soundness of speech that cannot be condemned so that those who oppose you may be ashamed because they have nothing bad to say about us.* –Titus 2:7-8 (NIV). Is there an opportunity for you to increase your level of integrity?

Integrity ensures you are above criticism.

• • •

4 Patience

A person's wisdom yields patience. –Proverbs 19:11(NIV). *Through patience a ruler can be persuaded*–Proverbs 25:15(NIV). *Patience is better than pride.* –Ecclesiastes 7:8(NIV). *Preach the word; be prepared in season and out of season; correct, rebuke and encourage—with great patience and careful instruction.* –1 Timothy 4:2 (NIV). *We do not want you to become lazy, but to imitate those who through faith and patience inherit what has been promised.* –Hebrews 6:12(NIV). *Brothers and sisters, warn those who are idle and disruptive, encourage the disheartened, help the weak, be patient with everyone.* –1 Thessalonians 5:14 (NIV). *But they that wait upon the LORD shall renew their strength; they shall mount up with wings as eagles; they shall run, and not be weary; and they shall walk, and not faint.* –Isaiah 40:31 (KJV). The Bible highlights many dimensions of patience as a character attribute, behavior, and tool linked to a reward.

Waiting in a business environment seems counterintuitive. People get paid to make things happen, not for waiting. However, chaos exists where there is no patience. Patience is the ability to endure, tolerate, be persistent, and otherwise stay the course when others may become discouraged (or quit).

Nobody likes to wait. However, we know that patience is a good thing. Patience contains the qualities of thinking and behavior modification. Imagine a patient person waiting in a room together with an impatient person. The mental picture that comes to my mind is clear—consider two interviewees arriving at 10 am for a one-hour appointment. The recruiter was paged at 10 am, the receptionist says the recruiter is on the way down, and it is now 10:15 am. One interviewee sits in a chair flipping through a business magazine. The second person is pacing, looking at his watch, and sighing. I get anxious just thinking about being around impatient people. Patience as displayed by the calm interviewee endures whatever it takes to be successful.

Although some might misinterpret patience as a lack of interest or weakness, it is a character trait that has lasting value. Interacting with people requires patience. Self-control requires patience. Completing ordinary tasks requires patience. Decision-making requires patience. Every facet of life calls us to be patient.

The subject of job promotion causes an alarming level of impatience in companies. People feel they are ready for the next job or next level and want it now. This impatient ambition causes people to obsess on the promotion and when it does not come, they become the victim. The victim behavior results in a bad attitude toward the leadership in the company or worse, an ultimatum—promote me or I will quit. *For I know the plans I have for you, declares the Lord, plans to prosper you and not to harm you, plans to give you hope and a future.* —Jeremiah 29:11 (NIV). God promises prosperity and has a unique plan for every person. Hard work is rewarded, and the timing is not always clear. Patience translates into continuing to contribute at a high level, being realistic about your readiness to assume the responsibilities of the next level, and understanding that when it is your time to get promoted you will be promoted.

I received my first promotion into vice presidency in 1998, and I thanked my group president. He told me there was no need to thank him. He shared that I was promoted from director to vice president because my level of performance was at the vice president level. He said, the promotion confirmed my contributions. It also meant that I still had to grow into the title but I had a head start based on a successful track record as a director. The promotion was also consistent with my stated career aspiration of becoming a senior vice president in operations. The next promotion came directly as a result of my patience. Two years later in 2000, I took a lateral move into a VP job which required relocation to North Carolina. Just three months later, a higher level VP job opened up that I was qualified for. I decided not to apply for the job because I had not proven myself in the lateral job, and I was having fun. I was willing to wait for the next time a higher level job opened. However, senior leaders in the company decided that I was the best person for the higher level VP job and recommended that I apply. I was offered the position. In summary, I was in the lateral job for six months and willing to stay longer. However, I had the skills to do the higher level job, and it was better for the organization that I move to the next level. This move also allowed another person in the organization to move up one level into my vacated position. Patience helped me and it will help you get to the next level and refrain from chasing a title. Someone is watching you prove your value and having conversations about a bright future with you on the team. Promotional conversations have a natural course, and we must be patient. Opportunities commensurate with your contributions will present themselves at the right time.

Patience is an advantage in life and throughout a career.

• • •

5 Compassion

Therefore, as God's chosen people, holy and dearly loved, clothe yourselves with compassion, kindness, humility, gentleness and patience. –Colossians 3:12 (NIV). *Be kind and compassionate to one another, forgiving each other, just as Christ, God forgave you.* –Ephesians 4:29 (NIV). *And the word of the LORD came again to Zechariah: "This is what the LORD Almighty said: 'Administer true justice; show mercy and compassion to one another. Do not oppress the widow or the fatherless, the foreigner or the poor. Do not plot evil against each other.'* –Zechariah 7:8-10 (NIV). God wants compassion to result in kindness between all people.

Compassion in the workplace supports teamwork and a culture of people helping people. Compassion can be defined with three C's— care, concern and consideration. It is expressed internally or externally toward another person or thing. Company leaders and working professionals have long shown compassion with philanthropic giving, food drives, and outreach programs during disasters like 9-11, earthquakes, hurricanes, tornados, fire, and death. Hospitals, like Cone Health in Greensboro, have compassion as a core value between healthcare professionals and patients.

Conversely, in some business models, needing help is taboo and showing compassion to someone needing help decreases the competitive edge. Some people inaccurately view needing help as a negative trait—incompetent, ill-prepared, inexperienced, and dependent. In the workplace, it's-all-about-me professionals will not spend any time helping a colleague. These professionals often hide behind rules to justify not being compassionate—not helping a woman struggling with a heavy box because of sexual harassment rules, not asking a person how he or she feels after a long absence from the office because of medical privacy rules, or not adjusting the work schedule by 15 minutes for someone that has a childcare issue because of schedule adjustment rules. Very little effort is required to show compassion—holding the door, moving out the way when maintenance is sweeping the floor, or giving someone a quarter in the cafeteria. These things do not get recognized in a staff meeting, the company newsletter, or on performance appraisals. Instead, viral word of mouth messages get shared about compassionate and uncompassionate people. Gestures of kindness earn the respect of others and can be a point of interest when leaders discuss your ability to manage relationships and leadership potential.

When making decisions about who to work for and where to work, a reputation of compassion is often a variable. People want to work with and for compassionate professionals. As I was making decisions about relocating from New York to a regional operating center for American Express, one of the factors was who I would work for. North Carolina came up on the radar and a woman I respected was the senior vice president. I knew and liked her but I needed more information. A trusted colleague provided me with additional details about her. She was smart, compassionate, and ambitious. Bottom line, the leader cared about her employees and was engaged in their development. I relocated to North Carolina to work for her, and she helped me to become a senior vice president.

Compassionate people need to be astute because compassion can be abused by others. Discerning between being compassionate and gullible requires good judgment and supporting data. As a SVP, I had to consider compassion and business performance. For example: when ice storms hit, the majority of people do not come to work or come in late. The expected compassionate message would be, "Be safe and please come in once the roads clear." On another occasion the threat of two inches of snow may cause people not to come to work. The compassionate message would say, "Please make every effort to be here for your scheduled workday and should it start to snow, we will make accommodations." Compassion is often adaptable to the situation and allows you to be authentic for the good of all constituents. *They said "if you will be a servant to this people, be considerate of their needs and respond with compassion, work things out with them, they'll end up doing anything for you."* –1 Kings 12:7 (The Message).

Compassion for others can lead to wise decisions.

• • •

6 Accountability

So we make it our goal to please Him, whether we are at home in the body or away from it. For we must all appear before the judgment seat of Christ, that each one may receive what is due him for the things done while in the body, whether good or bad. –2 Corinthians 5:9-10 (NIV). The first level of accountability is to God. Many significant and insignificant events elude the eyes of man but God knows our actions and holds mankind accountable.

For the ecosystems in businesses and communities to work effectively, people, systems, and processes have a level of accountability. Accountability is the obligation to report, explain, or justify something; to be responsible and answerable. In a business, the obligation to report personal and organizational effectiveness leads to accountability. Leaders explain their performance through 360-degree feedback from subordinates, peers and superiors. Employee metrics and controls detail performance results and ensure the organization operates as designed. Some accountability is automated; a report is generated that reconciles the actions of each employee. Other information is manually tabulated through quantified and qualified assessments of performance. Systems of accountability are designed to teach, improve performance, and identify negative outcomes before they erode performance. Accountability is solution-oriented and avoids finger pointing, assessing blame, and resurfacing issues. If we were all good and perfect, the subject of accountability would rarely surface.

Being accountable is parallel to taking ownership for your actions. There is no room for excuses or justification. People demonstrate accountability by bringing forward the unedited facts. Accordingly, rewards and consequences are issued based on results. Organizations are looking for people who will take ownership and control of their performance and business situations to achieve favorable outcomes. Taking ownership does not mean you directly took the action, caused the action, or even knew about the action. The action could be the result of a direct report, a vendor, a system, a fraudster, or another department. To take ownership one step further, fully accountable professionals will find solutions to problems they may not have caused.

My first presentation as a newly promoted senior vice president was a disaster. My team and I were working on a redesign for an incentive payment plan to employees with the assistance of a consulting firm. The initiative was going well, and it was time for an update to my boss and his boss. It was a great opportunity. The week before the presentation, my father-in-law died. I flew to New York for the funeral and left the writing of the presentation to the team. I planned on editing it and being fully prepared to present. I finally got an opportunity to look at the presentation in the airport as we were flying back from the funeral. The consultants had done a great job positioning the incentive plan. Upon arriving back in North Carolina, I settled my family and went to the office to ensure I would be ready for the presentation in New York the next day. The next morning, the airport security line was backed up, and I missed my plane. When I finally got to New York; the team was in the conference room ready to go. I kicked off the discussion but went blank on a page I did not fully understand. A sinking and sickening feeling immediately came over me. My ship was going down, and

I was alone. The questions from my boss felt like pins pricking my skin. I finally had to concede defeat and move to the next page. I was talking to keep the discussion moving yet consumed by my errors. When the meeting finally ended, I had to make the long trip from the conference room to my boss's office. The ensuing discussion was not pretty. I took ownership for not writing the presentation, not being prepared, and not admitting I did not know the answers to their questions. My leader was willing to give me a pass because of death in my family but I did not want a pass. I was fully accountable for not effectively representing the work. My next long journey was down the corridor to the other leader's office. I started with an apology. He told me it was not my finest hour but believed I recovered so we ended with a reasonable conversation on the topic. I asked for another opportunity to update them in 30 days. I was wrecked by nerves for the next 24 hours. I flew back to North Carolina and regrouped. Lessons learned—never delegate the full writing of a presentation to someone else, admit when you do not know an answer as soon as you realize you do not, and take time to mourn the death of a loved one. Taking accountability gives you credibility.

Additionally, accountability can cause you to intervene or take over broken processes. *"Am I my brother's keeper?"* –Genesis 4:9 (NIV). Recently, I learned of a group of girls with the potential to be good students but were distracted by behavior and academic challenges. A middle school counselor called me to help. Six girls and I took a journey to improve attitudes, self-control, and personal accountability. Every Monday morning we empowered each other to do the right thing without excuses. Participation was a benefit, and school suspension resulted in removal from the program. Not all of the girls made it through the program. The girls who did, learned how to be accountable—apologizing when they made a mistake, listening to feedback without talking back, accepting responsibility for their poor decisions to fight, attending school, wearing appropriate attire, and completing their school work. Most of all, these girls became accountable for their own success and self-control. The rates of suspension decreased for the group. Being accountable and influencing the accountability of others has led to extraordinary personal accomplishments. These girls have become my mentees and are now in high school.

We are accountable to God, self, and mankind.

• • •

7 Humility

For those who exalt themselves will be humbled and those who humble themselves will be exalted. –Matthew 23:12 (NIV). Humility takes the focus away from self and makes room for God and others to share the accolades.

Humility, the modest opinion or estimate of one's own importance, takes place before a career begins. *God opposes the proud but gives grace to the humble. –James 4:6 (NIV).*

Foregoing personal recognition in order for the team to win a minute in the spotlight is humility. Receiving a compliment because of your accomplishments and following up by acknowledging the hard work of the people behind the scene is humility. Declining an opportunity so that someone else can get the nod is humility. It is hard and nearly impossible to become successful in business and life without the help of someone. Humility allows you to acknowledge the contributors to your success. Success that avoids a self-centered attitude is honorable.

While on the road to success, humility prompts us to pause, give honor to God, and value our supporters. Arrogance ignores the prompt and speeds forward on its own merit to achieve more. Do you listen to the voice of humility?

Craving greatness is a never ending battle—professionals strive for victories bigger and better than the last. The consuming nature of a craving magnifies the desire to be more and do more. There is always something bigger and better than current status or possessions. The Bible suggests that we exchange reckless and arrogant desires for modesty, respectful competition, and gratitude. My source of humility is a humble beginning to life. Growing up in New York City public housing taught me modesty. Everybody is poor, and you share everything. We were a working class family with the same goals as suburban families. Buy a house, educate the children, and retire. At 13, my mother died, and my future became unknown. God stepped in, and my aunt adopted my two siblings and me. Death is humbling— there are many unfulfilled dreams in the cemetery. I live stable in my faith and grateful for every fulfilled dream.

As an internal auditor, I was making a name for myself as being competent, and I loved my job. I was getting excellent performance appraisals and felt like I was doing everything to get promoted. One day I learned that not only was I not going to get promoted but someone from outside the company was getting the job I wanted. If that was not bad enough, I was assigned to "show him around." Frankly, I was angry. I went in to see my leader and asked why I had not been told a job was open and secondly, why was I not considered as a candidate. He told me I was not ready to be promoted, and he wanted me to get more experience. I remember being so angry I had to leave the office and go for a walk. After a long weekend, I had to decide if I was going to work as a professional and show my new colleague around or was I going to make it hard for him. I decided to humble myself and accept that I did not get the job. My leader had the right to hire who he wanted. It was a tough few months in my career. I eventually got over it. I stayed with the department, the new guy got fired, and I got promoted. Humility can be a struggle when you think that you are smart and competent. It is important to not be overconfident and entitled. Are you willing to be humble and graciously accept what you cannot control?

The platform to exhibit talent is anchored by humility.

• • •

8 Passion

Elias was a man subject to like passions as we are and he prayed earnestly that it might not rain: and it rained not on the earth by the space of three years and six months. Again he prayed, and the heavens gave rain, and the earth produced its crops. –James 5:17-18 (KJV). Passion will focus the heart on specific actions to achieve specific goals.

Passion will influence career choices, work ethic, new ideas, and long-term planning. Passion is a powerful, compelling emotion or feeling; excitement and enthusiasm. Passion in the workplace can erupt into unbridled energy and become contagious as everyone unites toward a common goal.

Passion ignites faith and fearlessness to achieve a purpose. Symbolically, passion creates supernatural energy toward the aspiration. God facilitates new sources of energy when we passionately pray for His help and support. Passion can benefit from a dose of reality to ensure we have a rational perspective and properly address any obstacles.

Passion personified—wakes you up every morning to go to work, takes a red-eye flight to be present coast to coast, is a loud cheering section in your heart, is around-the-clock work effort, is exhausting hours of research, is a can-do attitude, and is unwavering faith. Passion can be the momentum that carries you to project completion. Passion is also a magnet that attracts people to each other for the benefit of inclusion, diversity, innovation, and creativity.

Realizing my passion took many years. I had a formal education in accounting, and I was a CPA—working with numbers was my gift. Contrary to my education, work experience, and credentials, accounting was not my passion. The road to discovering my passion meant self-examination of what gave me energy when I thought about it and what gave me energy when I was doing it. It was an accidental discovery of passion for me. I was working in risk management on projects that required me to develop strategies in collections and then implement them within our call center operations. I loved working with the training, marketing, technology, legal, and compliance groups, as well as the front line employees. I marveled at the integration of a good strategy and the measurable results. My passion centered on the analytical part of accounting and the energy was driven by making things happen with other people. The realization of passion meant that I could map a career for myself. Others could not set the course for my career and did not understand my choice in projects and lateral moves. The combination of analytical skills and teamwork produced a career change for me from accounting to operations management. My supernatural energy surfaced when I had the opportunity to lead large teams toward common goals and celebrate victory. I was blessed because I found and accepted my passion as my destiny. Had I known that operations management was in my future, I would have studied operations research. As God would have it, I studied accounting and my road to passion was different than others in operations management. The diversity of skills and backgrounds make the workplace a mosaic of education, experience, ambition, and passion.

Have you given yourself time to discover your passion? Are you willing to accept your passion or do you need others to validate your passion? What is your passion? Search until you find it.

My passions are my faith, my family, service to others, and motivating people to exceed expectations.

Passion speaks for you and about you.

• • •

9 Ambition

Make it your ambition to lead a quiet life; you should mind your own business and work with your hands, just as we told you, so that your daily life may win the respect of outsiders and so that you will not be dependent on anybody. –1 Thessalonians 4:11-12 (NIV). Paul's message to the Thessalonians suggested that ambition garnered respect because it built skills and led to independence.

Career ambitions built on the foundation of spiritual, family, organizational, and community successes make a well-rounded professional. Ambitious people champion their aspirations. They aspire to play a role of increasing authority in an organization. Ambition originates as an idea and quickly transforms into initiative and self-motivation. Organizations seek out ambition as a core competency in employees. Companies know that ambition is limitless. Winning cultures support and reward ambition.

Do nothing out of selfish ambition or vain conceit, but in humility consider others better than yourselves. –Philippians 2:3 (NIV).

Ambition benefits from humility. Unfortunately, some ambition is fostered by selfishness, greed, and corruption. Rigorous systems of internal controls safeguard against deviant ambition. Examine the latest corporate or community scandal at the root cause and usually, you will find a professional with good intentions and ambitions to be successful who takes a wrong turn onto Greed Boulevard. Avoiding the pitfall of greed relies on a personal code of ethics grounded by integrity. Is your soul for sale?

Young, smart, and ambitious are a great combination. How do you manage your ambition at 22 years old? First, set your moral compass—become rooted in a set of principles for what you will and will not do to be successful. Identify your passion. Design a plan to accomplish your career ambition linked to passion. Find mentors and sponsors who understand your goals. Make realistic plans to accomplish specific things in a specific timeline. Be prepared with an alternate approach should hurdles present themselves. Ambitious people—young and old—plan for the best and survive through the challenges.

Like most people, I consider myself ambitious. I pushed and worked my way through 25 years of career aspirations inside companies. Ambition led to long nights in the office, debates on the best approach to solve a problem, reengineering targets, international business travel, exposure to world-renowned business leaders, stock options, cash bonuses, and ultimately, the corner office. I have no regrets or apologies for my ambition. I do have moments that I am not proud of because I let selfishness get in the way a few times and called it ambition. I once developed a strategy to reengineer a process but did not get to implement the plan because I got promoted to another position. I was sitting in a meeting one day with a colleague, and she presented the plan I had left behind in my former group to our executive vice president. After the shock wore off, I was annoyed. My thoughts were "How dare she, that was my plan, and the least she could have done was redesign the presentation to make it her own." What was the real issue? Truth is, I wanted her to give me credit, and she did not. The reality was my old team had the plan, liked the plan, and owned the plan. They simply gave it to their new leader for the presentation. My ambition judged her ambition, and I felt I had integrity but she did not. The reality was we both had integrity. I let my ambition get in the way. I wanted to be recognized and get all the kudos. Is ambition clouding your judgment? Is ambition causing you to focus on what others are doing or not doing?

Ambition has an end point while integrity is enduring.

• • •

10 Wisdom

Do you want to be counted wise, to build a reputation for wisdom? Here's what you do: Live well, live wisely, live humbly. It's the way you live, not the way you talk, that counts. Mean-spirited ambition isn't wisdom. Boasting that you are wise isn't wisdom. Twisting the truth to make yourselves sound wise isn't wisdom. It's the furthest thing from wisdom. –James 3:12-14 (The Message). The book of Proverbs provides instruction for how we should live and contains numerous verses on wisdom. *Get wisdom, get understanding; do not forget my words or turn away from them.* –Proverbs 4:5 (NIV). *"I, wisdom, dwell together with prudence; I possess knowledge and discretion.* –Proverbs 8:12 (NIV). *For through wisdom your days will be many, and years will be added to your life.* –Proverbs 9:11 (NIV). *If you are wise, your wisdom will reward you;* –Proverbs 9:12 (NIV).

Wisdom connects intellect, emotions, and spirituality to formulate a gift from God for business and life. Wisdom is the state of being wise–knowledge of what is true or right coupled with just judgment as to action; discernment, or insight; scholarly knowledge or learning. Wisdom brings together diverse people, thoughts, and approaches to achieve business objectives.

The purpose for wisdom is to enlighten our character, thoughts, and behavior. It protects humankind from themselves and others. Wisdom is an accumulation of formal and informal education mastered through experience. An unofficial hierarchy exists for wisdom—young and junior-level professionals with less life and work experience have less wisdom, while the mature guru and senior-level professionals are expected to be wiser and pass wise insights to the next generation. Obviously this hierarchy is not always accurate. The world is full of wise youngsters and old fools.

Wisdom transforms thoughts and actions. Wisdom relays messages to the brain and heart from God. Your part is to allow wisdom to impart itself in you. Wisdom tells you what to say and do at the perfect time. Wisdom tells you the appropriate route to take and which routes to avoid when interacting with others. Wisdom provides structured decision-making criteria. Wisdom causes you to speak up and keeps you from inappropriately speaking. Wisdom evaluates the pros and the cons of career choices and timing. Wisdom encourages you to take a risk on yourself.

Wisdom has spoken to me, and I have listened most of the time. When I did not listen, I clearly recall the consequences. At 25 years old, wisdom told me to leave a job that did not address internal control issues. I did and had a wonderful career. At 40 and pregnant, wisdom told me to work differently and get more rest. I did not listen and spent 15 weeks on bed rest, most of them in a hospital room. At 47, wisdom told me to quit and spend more time with my husband, children, and God. I listened and am living the best years of my life. At 50, wisdom told me to write this book. I listened and await the response. In the workplace, wisdom has guided intellectual conversations, silence, and how to handle challenges. In community service work, wisdom has imparted patience, listening, and getting involved.

Wisdom is not a flashing light pointing you in the right direction. Wisdom takes assessing a situation to determine the best answer to a question or problem. I was faced with an aging technology that would break down periodically. I had two choices, make a multi-million dollar investment in new technology now or fix the existing technology to maintain a 20-year vendor partnership. The opinions were many and compelling. Very smart people weighted in on both sides. After several rounds of debate with colleagues and technology vendors, I had to make a decision. I combed over data, competitor feedback, vendor pitches, cost benefit analyses, and input from my team. I pulled the plug and went with a new vendor and new technology. As fate would have it, the old system broke one last time and could not be repaired. The timing was just as the new system was coming online. Wisdom was not emotional; it was factual and sometimes risky. The new system was not without its issues but it worked. The investment was a wise decision. Do you have the necessary information to make a wise decision? Do you understand the situation well enough to make a wise decision?

Wisdom is prudent and leads you in the right direction.

• • •

11 **Competitiveness**

It's true that some here preach Christ because with me out of the way, they think they'll step right into the spotlight. But the others do it with the best heart in the world. One group is motivated by pure love, knowing that I am here defending the Message, wanting to help. The others, now that I'm out of the picture, are merely greedy, hoping to get something out of it for themselves. Their motives are bad. They see me as their competition, and so the worse it goes for me, the better—they think— for them. –Philippians 1:15-17 (The Message). Paul warns those who believe in Christ that competition can drive people to do perverse things.

Being competitive is valued in business for its assertive approach to propel performance. Competitiveness is a desirable attribute. Competitive people invite competition. Competitiveness invites some to thrive and others to cheat. The upside of competitiveness allows cooperation, best practice sharing, innovation, creativity, efficiency, effectiveness, and awareness. Healthy competition will improve performance in an organization. On the flip side, the competitive nature of some people leads to adverse behavior creating errors and unfavorable results.

Competition is a misnomer between people on the same team and in the same company striving toward the same goal. A new word like *coopetition*—working together internally to compete against the external competition—reinforces expectations.

Competitive people generally make the team better. The natural instinct to win will push the team to its upper limits in terms of performance. Eventually, the team will break through and establish a new norm, which will be the high standard. Channeling competitive behavior toward the right target is essential. The target should be concrete but not a person, team, or department within the company. Competitive behavior focuses on triumphs through hard work, resilience, knowledge, ambition, humility, and integrity. Contradicting behaviors will attack, lie, steal, dictate, dishonor, and blame.

Competitive people engage in work, contests, and incentives to drive up the organization's overall performance based on individual contributions. Headlines featuring record-setting performance are usually the result of competitive individuals who push up the average performance for the whole team. Labels to be avoided include: overly competitive, competitive to a fault, mean-spirited competitor, not a team player, and dangerously competitive.

What management allows has a direct correlation on how competitiveness is executed. What gets measured gets done. The rules of competition in successful companies keep track of external competitors and endorse internal *coopetition* to improve total performance. Improvements in total performance can increase the market share of customers and industry revenue. Competitive cultures send a message of superior position through key words in the vision and mission statements—best, top, win, most, great, leader, extraordinary, better, and every. This sentiment of superior position ignites employees to achieve stellar results. High performing teams have a bond on the topic of winning which is the outcome of a competitive edge. Competitiveness fits into successful careers. Controlling the elements of competitive play is the collaboration between internal company controls and personal integrity. Internal controls and integrity act as safety nets should we get carried away with being competitive such as: inflated sales totals, overstated productivity statistics, fudged financial statements, overlooked customer complaints, regulatory compliance violations, and aggressive business tactics.

Today in the newspaper in Any City in Any State there is an article about victorious competitors and ill-fated competitiveness. Does your competitive edge help your resume?

My greatest professional and personal victories resulted in others being recognized. When Greensboro ranked higher than other locations in the company, we celebrated the results, teamwork, and quality of the work. The congratulatory e-mail was directed toward the spirit of competitiveness, competition, and *coopetition*. I wanted Greensboro to win in *coopetition* and in marketplace competition. I often reminded my teams that the competitor is not inside the company; we were all in the same boat and needed to row together to overtake our marketplace competitors. Financial incentives have always been motivators for promoting and rewarding competitiveness. Not keeping competitiveness under control has led to employees cheating by changing data or not properly completing a transaction. My own competitiveness is real and I play to finish the game with a win. My success was usually achieved through my employees. My competitiveness pushed people to get the job done. I reviewed reports daily, touched base with my direct reports to pace progress, held team conference calls to rally the troops, offered incentives to people willing to exceed expectations, and recognized excellence. The delicate balance of wanting to win and winning behavior meant constantly reminding employees about the code of conduct, immediately firing people who cheated, monitoring performance management reports, monitoring customer interactions for accuracy, and keeping my ambition in perspective.

A competitive spirit spearheads team victories before personal glory.

• • •

12 Perseverance

We know that suffering produces perseverance; perseverance, character; and character, hope. –Romans 5:3 (NIV). *Consider it pure joy, my brothers, whenever you face trials of many kinds, because you know that the testing of your faith develops perseverance. Perseverance must finish its work so that you may be mature and complete, not lacking anything.* –James 1:2-4 (NIV). *Take the old prophets as your mentors. They put up with anything, went through everything, and never once quit, all the time honoring God. What a gift life is to those who stay the course! You've heard, of course, of Job's staying power, and you know how God brought it all together for him at the end. That's because God cares, cares right down to the last detail.* –James 5:10-11 (The Message). The Bible offers clear examples of how staying anchored to faith brings a favorable conclusion.

Careers have great rewards, and they also have a downside of obstacles, adversarial relationships, and moments of fear. The downside can be resolved through perseverance and faith. Perseverance advances a course of action, or a purpose despite difficulties, obstacles, or discouragement.

Moses like Job stood in the face of adversity and won. *By faith he left Egypt, not fearing the king's anger; he persevered because he saw him who is invisible.* –Hebrews 11:27 (NIV). *Moses answered the people "Do not be afraid. Stand firm and you will see the deliverance the LORD will bring you today. The Egyptians you see today you will never see again.* –Exodus 14:13 (NIV).

Faith is the first element of perseverance. One must believe they deserve to reach the goal in order to achieve it. You must believe you can be a good vice president before setting out to become one, or a good business owner, or a good elected official, or the best candidate for a new job. Additionally, you must believe that the obstacles in a career will be diminished. Believe people who harass you will be removed, dishonest people will be caught, favoritism will be replaced with fact-based decision making, and wages below the norm will be increased.

Success may seem beyond the realm of possibility but faith, respect for reality, a plan, and perseverance can get you to the goal. Push toward the objective, purpose, and goal by allowing possibility and supporting information to determine the next steps. Maintain your credibility by being honest with yourself and do not become misguided by emotions. Is it reasonable to expect a promotion when you are only an average performer? Perseverance happens through empowerment. Establish a basis for your goals with data—have the ability to explain your case with supporting evidence.

With faith and facts on your side, it is time to persevere with the expectation of difficulty. Difficulty can be overt or subtle. Be prepared for resistance. Everybody wants to get to the next level in his or her career. When there is only room for one more at the next level, why should you get the position? Stand firm on the promise of God in Jeremiah 29:11 NIV *("For I know the plans I have for you" declares the Lord, "plans to prosper you and not to harm you, plans to give you hope and a future.")* with faith, facts, and perseverance. *Be on your guard; stand firm in the faith; be courageous; be strong.* –1 Corinthians 16:13 (NIV). Labeling the resistance from others with negative words like jealousy, incompetence, racism, sexism, favoritism, or stupidity, does not solve the problem. Avoid the distraction of labeling the actions of others and spend the time leveraging your faith, facts, and perseverance to get what God has for you.

After passing the CPA exam, I was required to submit a portfolio of work before licensing. My portfolio documented industry experience working under the direction of CPAs. The documentation process took months to complete. I was motivated by the prospect of being promoted because of this added credential. One of my colleagues was also putting together a package, and we would collaborate on some weekends to support each other. I finally finished my package. I gave it to my boss for review and the required sign-off. After several weeks, I asked about the status and was told—my package would be approved and submitted along with the package of my colleague once hers was complete. Without naming what I believed was unfair, I continued my job, and on November 19, 1990 I became a licensed New York State Certified Public Accountant. Today, the exact date of my license does not matter, but what matters is the act of perseverance to earn the title of CPA. It was undeniable that I could achieve my goal and prosper despite the delay in the process. I won in the end—delayed but not denied. *Forgetting what is behind and straining toward what is ahead, I press on toward the goal to win the prize for which God has called me heavenward in Christ Jesus. All of us, then, who are mature should take such a view of things. And if on some point you think differently, that too God will make clear to you.* –Philippians 3:13-15 (NIV).

Perseverance does not look back; it is faced forward and focused on conquering the obstacles ahead.

• • •

13 Generosity

Remember this: Whoever sows sparingly will also reap sparingly, and whoever sows generously will also reap generously. Each of you should give what you have decided in your heart to give, not reluctantly or under compulsion, for God loves a cheerful giver. And God is able to bless you abundantly, so that in all things at all times, having all that you need, you will abound in every good work. –2 Corinthians 9:6-8 (NIV). God is generous and sends messages for us to be the same. He has given to us, and we should happily give to others, whether it is with our money, our time, or our talent.

Generosity equates to high quality investments in people, on-the-job, and in communities. Professionals customize their level of generosity based on rational and emotional connections. Salaries, bonuses, and fringe benefits are rule-based decisions in most organizations and are not related to generosity. Most professionals are loyal to an organization for non-monetary reasons that equate to generosity.

Inevitably, generous people give based on relevance and passion. A sports fanatic will donate free time to coaching a youth sports team. A leadership enthusiast will speak without charging a fee to empower disadvantaged communities. An engineer will spend countless lunch hours with an elementary school robotics team. A reading specialist will donate books to elementary school children. *For where your treasure is, there your heart will be also.* –Matthew 6:21 (NIV). Generosity excites the giver through authentic expressions of care and it excites the receiver with the opportunity to experience an unearned reward.

Shallow obligatory giving will not yield anything for the giver or the receiver. Reluctant giving creates distrust and disconnects the recipient from the intended value. Attitudes of donors, volunteers, advocates, mentors, sponsors, and leaders can enhance or detract from the gift. Heartfelt giving plants a seed in the recipient that leads to the potential for a successful future. Take the colleague who is responsible for your on-the-job training. She shares her personal tip sheet and acronym list with you. She checks on you several times a day and is willing to answer all your questions. She offers to come in early and stay late if you need remedial instruction. She is a generous colleague. Any organization with a culture of people generously serving employees, customers, clients, and communities has the potential to generate tremendous loyalty.

When I relocated from New York to North Carolina for my career, I was without a support system. Once in North Carolina, my new boss would invite my husband, our young son, and me to her home for dinner on nights she wanted to make gourmet meals. We enjoyed her company, and it was very generous of her to support our family. She understood what it felt like to be new to a community without friends and family. Later, when I was on bed rest for 15 weeks, she came to see me in the hospital every week. Her generosity made Greensboro feel like home. My commitment to deliver results and loyalty to the organization was increased because of her generosity. My own generosity to others comes by extending a helping hand when people are looking for a job and sending an email to a hiring leader with my personal endorsement. It is demonstrated when I listen to career challenges and offer advice based on my experience. It is revealed when I volunteer to create a leadership development workshop for a not-for-profit organization. It shows when I make baked ziti for my son's friends to enjoy in the cafeteria at lunch time.

Generosity is heartfelt for the giver and the receiver.

• • •

14 Grace

The Lord said, "My grace is sufficient for you, for my power is made perfect in weakness." Therefore I will boast all the more gladly about my weaknesses, so that Christ's power may rest on me. That is why, for Christ's sake, I delight in weaknesses, in insults, in hardships, in persecutions, in difficulties. For when I am weak, then I am strong. –2 Corinthians 12:8:1 (NIV). In times of human weakness, God intervenes by adding more attributes to our character.

Grace manifests itself as composure when you are under pressure to deliver favorable business outcomes or when your career is off track. Grace is the influence, or spirit, of God operating in humans to regenerate or strengthen them. Grace is the elegance and beauty of manner, motion or action; a pleasing quality or endowment. Consider the grace you need to exhibit when you make a major error, and you are about to be fired. Grace is what you must demonstrate as you listen to a grousing employee who threatens to sue you for discrimination.

Grace is not a character attribute you talk about, but it is critical to have or acquire. The need for grace becomes compelling when you interact with someone who is graceless. Imagine the brute in the office who yells instructions, compliments, and talks before thinking.

Many times we just say these people have no class—when in fact, they have no grace.

Grace is equally available to rich and poor, college graduates and high school dropouts, gated communities and public housing residents, country club members and incarcerated inmates, as well as the exposed and unexposed. Grace relies on intuition and a connection with your core being. Intuition provides the barometers for right and wrong, good and bad, or proper and improper, while your core being keeps you calm and rational. The output is personified as the appropriate level of balance, self-control, acceptance, cordialness, concern, and competitiveness. Grace makes it look easy from the outside even though your stomach is in knots and your head is throbbing.

Grace allows God to intercede on your behalf when you are vulnerable. Grace creates an out-of-body experience that makes you look untouched by adversity and pressure. For example: Staying calm when being reprimanded for an accidental error in the workplace whether you caused it or not. *If a ruler's anger rises against you, do not leave your post, calmness can lay great offenses to rest.* –Ecclesiastes 10:4 (NIV).

During a transition of business responsibilities, I was in a meeting with colleagues and one of my bosses. The handover from me to someone else was underway. The new owner began to criticize my prior process while indicating he had a better solution planned. This went on for several hours. I just listened and responded to questions when asked. After the meeting, I was complimented for having grace. Reacting by standing on a table professing the perfection of my work or being defensive would not have changed the presentation or perception the new team wanted to make. My intuition and core being helped focus me on what was ahead and the bright spots in my life. I let it go and celebrated the victory as a leader with grace, and a new assignment.

Grace is a response and not a reaction under pressure.

• • •

15 Transparency

Jesus said to the disciples You can't keep your true self hidden forever; before long you'll be exposed. You can't hide behind a religious mask forever; sooner or later the mask will slip and your true face will be known. You can't whisper one thing in private and preach the opposite in public; the day's coming when those whispers will be repeated all over town. –Luke 12:1-3 (The Message).

God tested us thoroughly to make sure we were qualified to be trusted with this Message. Be assured that when we speak to you we're not after crowd approval—only God approval. Since we've been put through that battery of tests, you're guaranteed that both we and the Message are free of error, mixed motives, or hidden agendas. We never used words to butter you up. No one knows that better than you. And God knows we never used words as a smoke screen to take advantage of you. –1 Thessalonians 2:3-5 (The Message). The more transparent our actions become, the more support we will obtain from God and man.

Operating with transparency and candor, allows professionals and management to focus on generating trustworthy business results. Transparency is associated with the truth. Secrecy and acts of omission will sabotage careers, companies, and lives. Corporate policies and cultures must support the truth by disclosing information, assisting with investigations, and lawfully doing business. Professionals should conduct business with full disclosure and no hidden agendas. People directly impacted by a business transaction should have all the relevant facts. The transaction could range from why a process is changing to why the company is closing.

Perceived hidden agendas will impede business. Hidden agendas can be assumed when people do not feel like the internal message makes sense, the message contradicts previous messages, or when nothing is communicated. Every person in an organization can contribute to a culture of transparency. Transparency is supported by open and honest communication. When you cannot share information because of confidentiality, say that the information is confidential because of legal ramifications or too early to discuss, etc. When a decision has not been made, say no decision has been made, and we expect a decision within whatever timeframe applies. When change is introduced, tell people why change is happening. When a private meeting takes place in a public place, tell people why it was private. Transparency does not stop with the initial communication, it requires scheduled follow-up to address ongoing distractions.

My employees have put me on the spot in town hall meetings, in hallways, in staff meetings, and via e-mail. A direct question warrants a direct answer. Sometimes I was caught off guard but I always relied on the truth to respond. I tried to get in front of the rumor mill to stop the distractions. People always walked away with more information and occasionally dissatisfied with my direct response. I was once asked if layoffs were going to impact our region as the recession of 2007 was hitting. The answer was apparent but employees wanted to hear an answer directly from me. I was transparent with all the facts I had at that time (business was down) and preliminary discussions (no decisions had been made). The response they wanted to hear was no layoffs would happen because of the recession. That response was not realistic nor had any decision been made. I gave them enough information to think about but not overreact.

Transparency shares the facts in an authentic way.

• • •

16 Consistency

Jesus Christ is the same yesterday and today and forever. –Hebrews 13:8 (NIV). *Real wisdom, God's wisdom, begins with a holy life and is characterized by getting along with others. It is gentle and reasonable, overflowing with mercy and blessings, not hot one day and cold the next, not two-faced. You can develop a healthy, robust community that lives right with God and enjoy its results only if you do the hard work of getting along with each other, treating each other with dignity and honor.* –James 3:17-18 (The Message). God is the standard for consistency and what we can expect.

Companies derive benefits from employees that demonstrate consistently high performance. Being consistent starts with setting a pattern of what can be expected from you. Each day you are given an opportunity to perform consistent with your personal best. Business relationships function effectively when attitudes and actions are consistent with professional protocol. Consistency in your career builds your track record of success.

Paying attention to what you can control in your career allows consistent results. The controllable aspects of work include punctuality, following policy and procedures, positive relationships, and meeting deadlines. While most parts of your performance are controllable, there may be a few unexpected and uncontrolled issues that arise. The unavoidable disruption of technology outages, changes in policy, illness, and extreme weather, can adversely impact performance for a short period of time. However, on average and over time, these disruptions can be overcome with the consistency of good performance. Work to avoid patterns of mishaps and issues that may cause you to become unreliable. Mood swings in the workplace are an example of behavior that can make a professional unreliable. The consequence of inconsistency in the workplace can include low performance ratings, exclusion from high profile projects, negative feedback, and termination.

Consistency facilitates successful outcomes. Setting boundaries through standardized practices can alleviate extreme negative swings in performance. Standardized operating procedures for areas such as performance reporting, evaluation process, meeting structures, and process improvement; set the tone for consistency in the workplace. Establishing a precedent by not following the standardized process can bring chaos when the exceptions become the new rule for some and not others. Organizational boundaries need to then become personal guidelines we put in place to bring out our best performance. For example, develop a daily game plan for improvement based on the company's report of the prior day's results.

Consistency in my career resulted in becoming a reliable resource on the team. I came to work ready for my planned day but flexible enough to do whatever needed to get done. My title becomes worker or leader based on the need of the team. The reliability factor successfully influenced others to be likewise. Being reliable and flexible supported a culture of performance, problem solving, and developing people. Leading by example in the area of consistency ensured that employees and colleagues adapted attitudes and behaviors that would set the tone for the work environment. One area that I emphasize as my brand is a consistently positive attitude. I believe attitude is a game changer. I pride myself on people knowing what they can expect my attitude to be when they interact with me. On days when I am overwhelmed, tired, ill, or distracted, I ensure that people are not impacted through a grumpy or dismissive attitude from me. I encourage positive interactions and positive energy. I was in a board meeting and not sure I agreed with a direction the team had taken. I was disappointed that we were not looking to implement more integrated community solutions. Despite my opinion and concern, I ensured the quality of my interactions with everyone remained positive and productive. I later followed up for clarity and politely shared my concerns with the project coordinators. Can you isolate what you consistently do to improve performance or improve the work environment? Is your community or family improved by your consistency?

The mindset to consistently improve your contribution is valuable.

• • •

17   Discipline

Do you not know that in a race all the runners run, but only one gets the prize? Run in such a way as to get the prize. Everyone who competes in the games goes into strict training. They do it to get a crown that will not last, but we do it to get a crown that will last forever. Therefore I do not run like someone running aimlessly; I do not fight like a boxer beating the air. –1 Corinthians 9:24-26 (NIV). For the Spirit God gave us does not make us timid, but gives us power, love and self-discipline. –2 Timothy 1:7 (NIV). Like a city whose walls are broken down is a man who lacks self-control. –Proverbs 25:28 (NIV). God gives us the capability to exercise discipline as a matter of choice and courage.

Organizations expect professionals to be organized and disciplined as a minimum qualification for most jobs. Being disciplined helps you focus on completing the job correctly and meeting business goals. Discipline is the ability to focus on the desired outcome and avoid distractions. It requires self-denial and self-control. While discipline increases the probability of success, it is not a guarantee of success.

Exercise discipline when handling confidential information, managing deadlines, performing job functions, providing leadership, and keeping commitments. Discipline needs structure and personal commitment.

It realizes that scattered thoughts and actions decrease success. Disciplined people would not bypass established procedures to push a great idea into a new product offering without first using research and development guidelines. The disciplined professional working in a disciplined environment would follow the established process to maximize the potential for successful new product development. The revenue stream might take longer to be realized (in the disciplined approach) but is likely to be more sustainable.

Most of my career has been spent operating in rule-based functions like accounting and operations, where everyone and everything was subject to standardized and regulatory oversight. People not disciplined enough to follow rules were easily identified and subjected to the consequences. The notion of disciplined people and processes makes it easier for small and large organizations to predict financial outcomes and control variances. Random actions based on good intentions or ideas are not viable business models. Sustainable success can be achieved with disciplined performance as opposed to uncontrolled technical expertise.

My brain is wired in a very specific way when it comes to problem solving or issue resolution. A problem statement is the first step for me on most projects before I can take action or begin a discussion. In business, in the community, and in family matters, knowing the specific problem helps me to think. This discipline has saved time and frustration because it forces everyone to be aligned on the same exact problem to ensure the solution fits the problem. At United Way, we were reviewing statistics regarding the community and isolated high school dropout, incarceration, and teenage pregnancy as ongoing issues. The data suggested these issues were impacting African American males at alarming rates. We interviewed community leaders to qualitatively validate the data. Lawyers, judges, teachers, school administrators, business professionals, community volunteers, concerned citizens, and elected officials agreed that something needed to be done. The formulated problem statement was—the plight of some African American males. All solutions put on the table had to directly decrease the quandary of this population. The first solution put in place was a community-wide mentoring initiative with the ultimate goal of giving every male student a mentor. The mentor is designed to be an adult role model to positively impact the lives of the male students. The disciplined approach required transparency and focusing our attention on finding one solution at a time to address the problem. Many other solutions are under development but one important one is off the ground to address the problem statement.

Discipline will resist instant gratification in favor of long-term success.

• • •

18 Approachability

Live in harmony with one another. Do not be proud but be willing to associate with people of low position. Do not be conceited. –Romans 12:16 (NIV). In the final analysis, people are people, and all people should be respected regardless of status and titles.

When you are approachable, you show others that you are accessible. When you are accessible to others, it says that you are ready to receive the next new idea, suggestion for improvement, constructive feedback, as well as welcome the bad news in order to make corrections. Approachability sets the tone for how interactions between people throughout the company will happen or not happen. Approachability signals that the culture of the organization is inclusive and accepting of diverse perspectives and methods.

Being approachable spurs casual and formal interactions in the workplace. Approachable respects the chain of command but does not let the chain become a wall that hinders efficiency. Approachable says hello and does not look away when junior level people are walking toward you in the hallway. Approachable acknowledges emails from all levels and does not filter the inbox based on level. Approachable is relaxed and cordial in the cafeteria with everyone and does not look to lock eyes with peers in order to avoid others.

Unwritten business practices to prevent or limit junior-level employees from interacting with senior leaders are elitist. Closed doors will close off knowledge sharing, problem solving, and whistle blowing. Such organizations do not attract and retain open-minded professionals. Levelism can discriminate, discourage, and demean. People in an organization want access to leaders without being reprimanded or ostracized for asking a business question or appropriately speaking up. Some of my best suggestions for improvements have come from employees when I stopped to talk in the hallway, during roundtable discussions, during town hall meetings, and via email. Employees have shared the issues that cause customers to cancel accounts with the company. Employees have shared with me they want to personally get to know me and the other board of trustee members. These and other suggestions are only available if we make ourselves available to benefit from the contributions of all people.

Being approachable is a reflection of how I want to be treated. I am intentional about the treatment I extend to everyone from those who do the maintenance for my office up to the CEO. I make myself equally available to all people—neighbors, children, friends, strangers, new acquaintances, community leaders, elected officials, CEOs, etc. I try to refer to individuals by name during conversations. Title and position do not dictate with whom I will interact. My approachability allows employees to tell me the bad and good news. I asked employees to tell me about problems that needed to be fixed. One employee stood up in a meeting and told me that when she tried to transfer a customer call from one department to another, the receiving department refused to take the call. On another occasion, an employee came to tell me he was not receiving performance management support such as periodic updates and annual feedback. Some of these issues were going on for years but nobody was talking about it. People did not fear retaliation for responding to my request to make the workplace better by addressing real issues. People often refer to "feeling comfortable" or "feeling safe." Professionals have cried in front of me and trusted me to help them. Approachability is not a banner but it is ever present and sensed. I love my approachability because it gives me access and permission to connect with people to celebrate improvements or address problems.

On the flip side, I have been approached by people who are aggressive. Honestly, it can be startling and cause you to avoid further interactions. Physical touch by people I do not know, loud talking, asking personal questions, and being rude are examples of approaches that turn me away. I try to give everyone a second chance or give them feedback on why their approach was not effective. Employees who called me after being terminated were usually not connected to my direct line, and they were told they needed to work with the human resources department on any lingering issues. Customers who called me were always welcome to explain their issue directly but if it was threatening or verbally abusive, I did not take those calls or I warned customers the call would be terminated if the abusiveness continued. Sometimes you must know when an interaction is a no-win situation.

Approachable people create a comfortable, inclusive, and improvable environment.

19 Strength

Although the Lord gives you the bread of adversity and the water of affliction, your teachers will be hidden no more; with your own eyes you will see them. Whether you turn to the right or to the left, your ears will hear a voice behind you, saying, "This is the way; walk in it." –Isaiah 30:20-21 (NIV). Listen and follow God's voice to find wisdom and strength.

A bad day at work is guaranteed. How you work through the bad day is a matter of strength. Adversity and affliction offer the choice to live with a situation or grow through it. The stresses of life and career create two possible outcomes—become the victim or become the survivor. The ability to survive is dependent on finding the strength to have a positive attitude in adversity and direct actions toward improving the situation. Becoming the victim consumed with self-pity is easy when a project fails, a major client stops doing business with you, or you are terminated from a job. The right of survivorship requires strength through emotional and intellectual composure. Allow your rational and spiritual voice to offer guidance. The mind must be trained to look beyond an extreme situation for viable responses. A reasonable path to survival may require prayer, professional counseling, medical treatment, and support groups. *I can do all things through Christ which strengthens me.* –Philippians 4:13 (KJV).

The biblical context for bread and water in contrast to adversity and affliction in the opening scripture above tells us that all four are part of every life. The human body gets strength from bread and water to prepare it to survive adversity and affliction. Survival is possible no matter how bad it gets at work or at home. Put your feet on the floor to move forward—the road to survival will not be easy, fun, or short. *So do not fear, for I am with you; do not be dismayed, for I am your God. I will strengthen you and help you; I will uphold you with my righteous right hand.* –Isaiah 41:10 (NIV). How do you find strength when adversity appears?

One of my most personal adversities impacting work happened in 1996. I got promoted, engaged, married and pregnant all in a 12-month period. I was at peace and happy with life. During a routine doctor's appointment, I had a second trimester miscarriage. My husband and I were devastated. Why me? I was a good Christian and doing good things for the community. I was depressed and immobile for many weeks. My boss called me regularly to offer encouragement. I had to pray, seek counseling, and get back to work with positive productive people. I will never forget my adversities and I am stronger because of the bad days.

Strength is a signal that God is with you and is helping you.

• • •

20 Curiosity

After three days they found him in the temple courts, sitting among the teachers, listening to them and asking them questions. Everyone who heard him was amazed at his understanding and his answers. —Luke 2:46-47 (NIV). Jesus as a young boy gained wisdom out of his curiosity.

Professionals seeking new information and answers to questions are intellectually curious. Supportive corporate cultures encourage questions. It takes courage to ask the first question in a room, question the leader, and question the status quo.

Curious people have the courage and intelligence to ask questions and then listen to the answers. Pretending to know something or not caring enough to want to know something defies our natural instincts. The mind is always at work to understand new input. Curiosity is naturally stimulated through sight, sound, smell, touch, taste, and emotion. Typically we see or hear something that intrigues us to learn more about the subject.

When you raise questions, a nonintrusive technique is a win-win situation. An accusatory style puts people on the defense and blocks the free flow of information. Rhetorical questions may make people suspicious because answers are presupposed. Many times rhetorical questions can expand or confirm your knowledge on a subject matter. One successful technique for asking questions begins with telling people why you are asking the question—I want to apply for a position in your department, would you mind if I ask you a few questions about what you do? However, you should avoid asking questions you already know the answer to—the last day to apply for the job was yesterday, can I apply now?

You will be rewarded and recognized when the meaningful information that you possess translates into value for the organization. Conversely, as adversity arises, others may question what you should know. For example, a leader should know if the organization is running into a deficit because expenses are more than revenue. This fact should be known before the deficit occurs. Not knowing because the finance person did not tell you is not a good explanation. Often professionals make the mistake of operating with blinders on which projects an attitude of "that's not my job," or indifference. Other times, colleagues do not tell you what you should know. How do you address the "need to know" bias of others?

Be intellectually curious about matters beyond your job scope because it can impact you. Countless professionals get fired for what they should have known or what they should have detected. Ask questions, look at reports, get feedback, respectfully look over the shoulder of colleagues, welcome internal auditors to review your process, put in internal controls, follow-up on suspicious activity, and learn as much as you can about as much as you can.

Early in my career, I did not ask enough questions. I left meetings not completely sure of next steps. After the meeting, I would limp my way through or ask somebody a few follow-up questions. I often assumed that I was the only person who had questions and did not want to look like the odd-ball or prolong the meeting because I had questions. One day I stayed behind after a meeting and asked my senior vice president a few clarifying questions which he was happy to answer. I soon began to realize that my colleagues had unanswered questions. I created an approach that I use even today. I write down my questions as they come up. I wait for all information to be shared. Should any unanswered questions remain, I ask in the meeting or quickly send a follow-up email or meeting request. Closing the knowledge gap increases my effectiveness.

Curiosity means you know enough to know you need answers to questions.

• • •

21 Courage

Preserve sound judgment and discernment . . . go on your way in safety, and your foot will not stumble; when you lie down, you will not be afraid; when you lie down, your sleep will be sweet. Have no fear of sudden disaster or of the ruin that overtakes the wicked, for the LORD will be your confidence and will keep your foot from being snared. –Proverbs 3:21-26 (NIV). *I will not be afraid. What can man do to me?* –Proverbs 118:6 (NIV). Courage comes out of trust in God, confidence, putting aside fear, and the use of good judgment.

Courage causes people to put aside fear to move in their career or business venture not knowing what lies ahead but hoping for the best. Courage will branch out to do something new or unexpected to attract a new opportunity. People are labeled as courageous based on the viewpoints and observations of others. Sometimes it takes the acknowledgment of others to affirm your status of courage. Courageous people do not set out to be honored. These people take an action because it feels like the appropriate thing to do. For example: being the single person to disagree with the direction the team is taking because you have technical and expert knowledge that the team recommendation has hidden costs and is prone to errors. You tactfully oppose the approach by presenting a more cost effective, contemporary, and efficient solution without berating the team recommendation. Being courageous takes patience to give others time to think and rethink. The courage of one person can influence current and future behaviors of observers.

Fear can dominate all action and freeze a career or life. Fear has a voice that says "I'm 45; I could never go back to school." Or it may whisper "I should not apply for that job because I could never do as good a job as others." It may even tell you "I should just go along with the group to avoid constructive confrontation." While some people are frozen by fear, others are moving ahead. Standing still in a career or life is equal to moving backward. As the gap gets wider, the person standing still becomes obsolete.

Courage sees the limitless possibilities God offers in the world. Courage takes control by walking away from fear and lunging toward faith, a new job, new skills, enacting change despite resistance from colleagues, relocating, following company policy without shortcuts, and self-confidence. The day I announced my departure from American Express, I received e-mails from across the company congratulating me on my decision and telling me I was courageous. At first, I could not reconcile bravery to my decision to devote my full attention to supporting my family. I ended my SVP role at American Express because my 5-year-old daughter, 10-year-old son, and loving husband needed me more than I needed American Express. To be honest, I had tremendous fear and trepidation about leaving behind 25 years of corporate experience. I was afraid of the financial implications, my future value in the marketplace, loss of status in the community, and limited shopping sprees. My moment of truth came one day while on the beach at 6 am. I was praying for peace because internal turmoil kept me awake at night challenging my decision to resign. My prayers were answered. I received peace and clarity. Success was less about a title at a specific company—it was more about using my intellectual capital differently. Money and the fear of not having it held me captive—it was necessary to unlock the platinum handcuffs, leave my career, and let life happen. I replaced fear and guilt with the full-time and awesome gift of a family.

Have courage to take control of your career and life with confidence in your faith and competencies. What is courage asking you to do?

Courage conquers legitimate fear and doubt.

• • •

22 Optimism

But as for me, I will always have hope; I will praise you (Lord) more and more. My mouth will tell of your righteousness, of your salvation all day long, though I know not its measure. –Psalm: 71:14-15 (NIV). We wait in hope for the LORD; he is our help and our shield. In him our hearts rejoice, for we trust in his holy name. –Psalm 33:20-21 (NIV). Optimism projects positive energy.

Is optimism the assumption that things will go well, that hard work will be rewarded, and that nothing but death is irreversible? Optimism can be the hope that misfortune will not come and if it does, it is resolvable. Where there is a sliver of hope, optimistic people find it. Optimistic professionals attract attention to their work. People are always interested in an upbeat work environment. Optimism is attracted to what is going well and is less reactive to the deficiencies of people or surroundings. Being optimistic makes you part of a rare group that quickly calculates the odds of something good coming out of a grim situation.

Optimism is aware of reality and chooses to exert energy on favorable endings. Several people talk about hope as a part of spiritual lessons, speeches in business, advice from friends, slogans, and personal reflections. Do these people project optimism? Optimism comes across in our attitude toward other people, toward a work effort, or toward an environment.

Optimism kept me level-headed during numerous reengineering efforts in various areas I have worked. There was always a risk that I might lose my job but I never became preoccupied with being unemployed. I had conversations with peers during these times of uncertainty about skills—what transferable skills did I have? The one skill I found very necessary was the ability to get projects implemented on time and in budget with the expected financial benefit. I exploited that skill for many years. The topics ranged from new debt collection practices, new technology implementation, new letter design, new internal audit processes, managing balance sheet exposure, incentive redesign, process elimination, etc. I stayed hopeful that after implementing necessary process improvements, a position requiring my skills would be part of the new structure. I was optimistic and positioned myself as an asset through my prior contributions and potential future value. I believed in my skills and that God was going to provide work opportunities.

Optimism can fix the problem to prevent the issue from becoming a big deal.

• • •

23 Presence

And Jesus grew in wisdom and stature, and in favor with God and man. –Luke 2:52 (NIV). Do your best to present yourself to God as one approved, a worker who does not need to be ashamed and who correctly handles the word of truth. –2 Timothy 2:15 (NIV). Presence creates an image that reveals to people without a spoken word that you have authority, wisdom, and grace.

A positive or negative presence can impact the perception others have of your ability to take on greater responsibility in the company. Presence has become a desirable character attribute. In more recent times, *presence* has evolved to include executive-level presence. Do you have what it takes to be an executive—composure under pressure and the ability to balance demands from the public? The interpretation may vary from organization to organization and person to person; simply, presence is how you show up.

Presence is subjective, physical, and behavioral. To have or not have presence is a question of what the majority of the decision makers think about how you present yourself. The subjective nature of presence requires that you are cognizant of the expectations of others. Some will say that it is discriminatory to indicate that presence has anything to do with your physical appearance. Presence does have something to do with how you look. Describe the last person you saw promoted. Have you ever seen an unattractive, untraditional, inappropriately dressed, or untidy executive on the cover of an annual report, magazine, or in front of employees in a town hall meeting? The last element of presence is behavioral. The behavior associated with presence is what you are observed doing. That behavior may be extrapolated as what you will do when nobody is watching. Your observed behavior in meetings is assumed to be what you will do or say in response to similar situations. Fair or not, if you are boisterous on Monday in front of your leader, it is assumed you will be the same in all meetings. Showing up prepared and calm in a meeting with your leader after your previous boisterous appearance can start to unravel negative perceptions of your presence. Building presence happens over a period of time. Presence is supported by shared observations from peers and leaders. You are what people perceive. Does your presence reflect your character attributes and personal conduct? Look in the mirror, listen to your words, and observe your actions to measure appropriateness for yourself.

The expected attire at a business meeting along with being prepared to discuss a specific topic with data, curiosity, and confidence can be the beginning steps to establishing your presence in an organization. A lack of presence or mixed reviews about your presence does not prevent you from getting a bonus, but it might inhibit your assignment to the big projects and getting promoted. How effectively do you handle an assigned task?

Presence is not flashy or overbearing. It is authentic and natural. Some people have to work to have presence while others have an innate presence. I developed presence by combining my God given gifts with lessons learned from observing leaders I respect. It takes time and practice for your presence to evolve to a point that it is recognizable and appreciated. Early in my career I was goofy, and I tried too hard to please everybody. I evolved by depending on faith to give me insight. I started to show up differently. I dressed like the more senior level women in the firm and not like my peers. What others thought about me was not a priority. Instead, I focused on getting the job done and being respected and respectful.

I take copious notes and review them after meetings for key facts and action items. I ask questions, listen to the response, and take informed action. I establish commitments with others for deadlines. I give credit to others who contribute to success. I build relationships and respect authority. In summary, my presence is felt by a broad range of constituents within the appropriate boundaries.

Presence is the blend of your character and work ethic interpreted by others.

• • •

24 Servant

I am your servant; give me discernment that I may understand your statutes. –Psalm 119:125 (NIV). *Your attitude should be the same as that of Christ Jesus: Who, being in very nature God, did not consider equality with God something to be grasped, but made himself nothing, taking the very nature of a servant, being made in human likeness. And being found in appearance as a man, he humbled himself.* –Philippians 2:5-7 (NIV). Servants have the willingness to submit to the guidance of God and recognize the purpose of His directions.

Servants in business yield to the directions and needs of superiors, peers, and subordinates as an act of respect, humility, and trust. Servants do whatever needs to get done to strengthen the organization, community, or person. They recognize that good ideas and instructions can come from a host of sources and are not exclusive to senior level executives. Servants put aside personal pride and preferences to serve others. Servants are defined by their hearts. The heart of a servant is inclusive and values all people. As such, a servant submits wholly to the concept of being used wherever needed to make an impact.

Some service is for direct compensation. Even when being paid, the heart of a servant has an intent and purpose beyond getting money. Other servants volunteer to serve for the pleasure of seeing others succeed and objectives met. The reason for a servant's work is often to affirm the value of people, create harmony, get everyone thinking bigger, increase the contributions of each team member, and collectively make a lasting impact. A servant surveys the need, anticipates challenges, and finds solutions. The servant may accomplish his or her work with and through others or as a one-person team. A servant might work late to give the minor but needed data to a colleague to complete the project and steps into the background while others get the public recognition. Servants want everyone on the team to rack up a win. In addition, they help others find the lesson in the losses. A servant gets joy from the small victories that may or may not lead to big accomplishments. For example, big accomplishments such as tutoring a student in reading but the student does not improve. However, you refer the situation to the school, and the student gets tested for increased educational services. Ultimately, the student is on the way to getting remedial education to address the basic skills necessary to read.

During moments of defeat, a servant is like an emergency response team. A servant will let you lick your wounds for a minute or two but he is more interested in closing the wound, and restoring your strength. Service to others in adversity gets the adrenaline flowing and the mind thinking about new partnerships, new processes, new data, restoring confidence, making others self-sufficient, learning from experience, transformation, solving the problem, and creating a new set of servants. In the worst of times, a servant comes to the forefront. Hurricane Katrina in 2005 is an example of men, women, and children helping the families of New Orleans in a disaster based on need and compassion. There are also examples in the workplace when people make a meal for the family of a colleague who is in the hospital or walk in a fundraiser to support a co-worker who has a child with juvenile diabetes.

The relationship between a servant and those being served may be one-sided. A servant will act out of love for mankind while recipients might be ungrateful, indifferent, greedy, unengaged, disrespectful, entitled, uninspired, and apathetic. Being a servant does not mean you get dumped on or get the dirty jobs. However, you might get some of the unpopular work. The recognition for servants might be less than what others get, or it can be equal or even greater. In all cases, the experience of a servant has a long-term reward in terms of community and workplace impact, as well as positive influence on the recipient. The compounding effect of small acts of service are the cornerstones of most communities—churches, organizing senior citizen groups, neighborhood watch members, rotary clubs, Bible study fellowship, parent teacher associations, hospital volunteers, food pantries, soup kitchens, mentoring, tutoring, and coaching.

In the final analysis, a servant yearns for the success of others. There is an emotional and almost irrational compulsion to do something good for others that is healing and empowering. The servant does more than a superficial act—servants give a shirt to the shirt-less, to restore self-respect and confidence for a job interview. Have you ever helped someone as an impulse without thinking first? The character of a servant is compassionate, humble, optimistic, courageous, authentic, generous, strong, and patient.

Being a servant started by observation for me. I watched my mother serve others at church. She was an usher, baked cakes, and visited the sick. I then became the recipient of the good work of servants in Sunday school, girl scouting, and when my mother died, her co-workers at the post office gave us back-to-school clothing. As an adolescent, I continued to benefit from servants who were volunteers in Junior Achievement, cheerleading coaches, and neighbors giving me a ride from place to place. I received the gift of confidence, self-respect, basic needs, education as a priority, and the desire to serve. Over the last three years, I have ramped up my service and dedicated myself full time. The affiliations and organizational names are not important. What stands out as my servant opportunity is helping to restore basic needs in my community, giving people hope, showing love to a stranger, teaching a child to read while reinforcing she can do anything, mentoring to influence positive behavior, and being satisfied that at least one person will have a better life because of my service. The workplace opportunity is the same as the community opportunity. A colleague needs your help with job tasks, project deadlines, report writing, strategy development, data gathering, employee development, public speaking, confidence building, a sick child, or perhaps, elder care recommendations. Do you know the needs of your colleagues, friends, or community? Are you willing to ask how you can serve others? What are you going to do to serve?

Servants offer their skills to make others better.

• • •

25 Personal Brand

The Son is the radiance of God's glory and the exact representation of his being, sustaining all things by his powerful word. After he had provided purification for sins, he sat down at the right hand of the Majesty in heaven. So he became as much superior to the angels as the name he has inherited is superior to theirs. –Hebrew 1:3-4 (NIV). Jesus is the exact representation of God. He lived up to the expectation of godliness and is now seated at the right hand of God in heaven.

Brands represent organizations in the marketplace. These brands attract professionals in search of a work culture consistent with the messages relayed in the brand story. Examine elements of your favorite brand. Does it represent innovation, fun, wealth, a winner, smart people, quality, and globalization? Can you see how your personal aspirations might be consistent with the story of that organization? Would you want to work for one of your favorite brands if given the opportunity? Organizations spend millions to build a brand which makes a direct and subliminal impression with a target audience. Likewise, individuals build a personal brand to represent their potential contribution to an organization. Resumes are the common story board for personal brand messages. Social media has changed the playing field and now good and bad brand messages can reach potential customers and employers.

Personal brand is determined by an individual. Building a personal brand is an exact representation of all your character attributes and your performance. People have an expectation that you will live up to your brand messages—personal best, resumes, social media, reputation, and word of mouth. Today, it is not only important to create a brand but also to control the brand. Controlling your brand happens by containing communication to intended audiences and living your brand at all times. Personal brand management is hard work, and it never stops. Nothing is private, confidential, or off-limits in our web-enabled and imposing society. Brand does not have the benefit of a personal interaction. Brand often precedes people just as the brand of a product usually precedes your experience with the product.

In the Bible, Ruth's favorable reputation preceded her. *All the people of my town know that you are a woman of noble character.* –Ruth 3:11 (NIV). What is your brand inside of your company or in the external marketplace? What are people saying about you before you enter the room?

Only God and Jesus are perfect. Accordingly, understand that you will make mistakes and as part of brand management, you will need a recovery plan. Some attributes that will assist you with recovering from an error in judgment or failed performance include humility and accountability. Apologize for your errors and take responsibility for your mistakes. Next, fix the problem and move on to avoid dwelling on mistakes.

Brands evolve, as well as reverse course. The evolution of a brand can be linked to experience—from a junior-level professional with little experience to a seasoned leader with global experience. Brand reversal can move from good to bad or vice versa. An outstanding employee is now the subject of a federal fraud investigation. The average employee was previously viewed as not being a strategic thinker, is given a new project where he or she demonstrates strong strategic outcomes through innovative product development and implementation. Again, it is hard work but worth the effort to solidify your brand in the workplace, community, and to potential employers. Your personal brand ties together facts, opinions, your character, demonstrated behaviors, and your accomplishments.

My brand is still evolving through the various stages of my life. I guard my brand to avoid misinterpretation and abuse. God gave us Jesus as a brand to aspire toward. Although we will never get to that brand recognition or storyboard, we can strive to have a character more like Christ. My personal brand messages vary from day to day based on the circumstances. However, some brand messages that I have on my permanent list are—Christian with strong leadership skills, integrity, and a servant's heart.

I did not submit my resume to American Express in 1987 thinking about brand. I just wanted a job with a global company to gain great experience. Nor did I decide to leave the company based on my brand. However, my brand was shaped by both events. We only get one chance to make a first impression and one chance to make a last impression. How many brand messages do you create? Are the messages and impressions intentional? Do you create opportunities to share your brand message? Can you identify the brand messages in the following story?

My last day as an employee of the American Express Company was April 27, 2009. The day marked the 2009 Shareholders Meeting and Board of Directors Meeting hosted in Greensboro, North Carolina. Although I had decided to exit my career with the company, I proactively committed to making the meetings a success for the employees and the leaders. We worked around the clock for several weeks planning and perfecting the events. We would showcase community engagement, employees, innovation, customer care, and leadership. On Sunday, April 26 my last impression started to take shape. The Sunday evening agenda was a dinner with the Board of Directors highlighting a community project and partnership. I began the meetings with a story at dinner about leadership and service intersecting in my personal and corporate life. In 1960, my mother and father left the segregated south to seek opportunity and employment in New York City. Simultaneously, on February 1, 1960, four freshmen of NC Agricultural and Technical State University asked for a cup of coffee at a local Woolworth lunch counter in an effort to integrate the lunch counter and combat racial inequality. As my first external philanthropic act after becoming the leader in Greensboro, American Express Company made a significant financial investment supporting historical preservation and leadership—The International Civil Rights Center and Museum in Greensboro and the location of the 1960 sit-in movement.

A civil rights legend, Mr. Franklin McCain, was at the dinner to share the story as one of the four young men who asked for a cup of coffee at the Woolworth lunch counter. I had an intellectual and emotional rush of 21 years of service to one company and my birth right all come together in one place. In 1960 I would have been unable to eat at a Woolworth lunch counter and in 2003 I became the first African American woman to preside over the operations in Greensboro. My humble beginnings, character, workplace performance, passion for people, desire to serve, and blessings from God helped me to give thanks for the platform I had been given and say goodbye at the same time.

The next day was ethereal, the climate was joyous, employees were spectacular in presentations, intellectual stimulation was visible, and the world seemed to stop moving for a moment. I saw the beginning and the end of a major part of my life. The CEO paused to thank me for my service and accomplishments. The employees supported and appreciated my service with messages of thanks. I was honored to serve my employees and a company I loved. There could not be a better last day of service to a company that taught me so much. The leaders of the company got to experience my passion for the community and what my leadership of 2,500 great employees had produced. At 5 pm the jet's wheels were up, the day was done, and I removed my name from my office door. I walked to the parking lot at peace and grateful.

My personal brand in the role was cast (as a first impression for some and the last impression for most) and the event recorded in the history of the company. Today, I am in a new chapter of my brand building. it is an image of blessings, prayer, gratitude, miracles, education, family, friends, thoughts, dreams, experience, and aspirations.

A personal brand radiates intentional messages.

• • •

This ends the section on character attributes. Our character should not be defined by education and job training. Character is the moment we let our faith act as a guide to fulfill the peaceful loving plan God has for us. Many of the 25 attributes may already be in your portfolio but *The Next Level* is a plea for you to connect attributes and faith. Upon the connection of the attributes, our personal brand becomes visible. Who we are becomes a story of purpose and not a compilation of titles from a company. Connect the dots of your character attributes to establish a foundation to build your life and career upon. Strive to get to The Next Level with God as your guide. Take time to reflect on each of the 25 attributes as an expectation and opportunity to celebrate you! *God's grace is sufficient.* –2 Corinthians 12:9 (NIV).

• • •

SECTION II

The focus of the next 25 chapters is to keep you on track by using character to drive up your performance. We will move from just doing your job to making an impact that improves business results. Being able to measure your value through results related to your performance is the bottom line in business. A Hierarchy of Performance is built on the foundation of character. The hierarchy helps to compartmentalize expectations as you advance inside of your career. The tactical layers of performance are linked to 50 biblical scriptures and described in three categories:

Fundamental   basic behaviors expected from a professional.
Accelerators   intermediate level ideas, thoughts and actions
                  associated with professionals likely to be promoted
                  or receive increasing levels of responsibility.
Breakthrough   advanced abilities that create strategies, innovate,
                  and increase business impacts associated with
                  seasoned and senior professionals.

Section II goals:

1. Link biblical scripture to conduct at work.
2. Set performance expectations.
3. Offer examples of strong performance.
4. Provide a call to action.

HIERARCHY OF PERFORMANCE

BREAKTHROUGH

Transform
Inspire
Lead
Connect The Dots

Make A Decision · Take Risks ·
Lead & Follow · Give Back ·
Improve The Culture · Prioritize ·
Manage Relationships · Influence

ACCELERATORS

Be Excellent · Market Your Story · Create A Plan ·
Think · Focus On The Goal · Communicate · Ask
For Help · Increase Knowledge · Do More · Resolve
Conflict · Gather Data · Collaborate · Follow Protocol

FUNDAMENTALS

Faith · Authenticity · Integrity · Patience · Compassion · Accountability ·
Humility · Passion · Ambition · Wisdom · Competitiveness · Perseverance ·
Generosity · Grace · Transparency · Consistency · Discipline · Approachability ·
Strength · Curiosity · Courage · Optimism · Presence · Servant · Personal Brand

FOUNDATION

The doer of God's word is blessed in his doing.

—James 1:25 [paraphrased]

"What you do today is training for *The Next Level*."

26 Be Excellent

Whatever you do, work at it with all your heart, as working for the Lord, not for men. –Colossians 3:23 (NIV). *The service of Hezekiah was good, right, faithful, obedient, and he worked wholeheartedly. As a result, he prospered.* –2 Chronicles 31:20-21 (NIV). Excellence requires engaging the heart in whatever you pursue.

Careers begin with the outlook that personal excellence at work will result in success. Three considerations to support excellence include: excellence is intentional, leadership is embodied in excellence, and it only takes one person at a time to create excellence. These three elements of excellence apply whether you are volunteering or getting paid to excel. Excellence has tangible benefits. In a marketplace of choice, excellence and quality attracts employees, customers, and profits.

Respected and successful professionals are expected to be excellent at their jobs. Let's examine the elements of excellence starting with intention—first, people make a conscious decision to be engaged, committed, accurate, and solution-oriented. Excellence is the result of a person's deliberate and best effort. Similarly, 1 Peter 4:10 (NIV) states *each of you should use whatever gift you have received to serve others, as faithful stewards of God's grace in its various forms.* Conversely, we all have experienced the bad service of a dismissive person or a colleague who contributes minimum effort on the project.

Second, excellence means taking a leadership role to control performance. The mindset to excel is innate—people who pursue excellence are born, not trained. Corporate development and training will bring to the surface an individual's natural characteristics toward winning with the highest quality possible. People with leadership tendencies have a natural instinct to figure out or seek out the best answer.

Third, the delivery of excellence is an independent decision for each person involved in a transaction. The contribution and attitude of one person at a time can create an excellent outcome. In other words, we should seek excellence regardless of the choices being made by people around us. Choose excellence when others choose to be average, to do as little as possible, or to completely avoid doing work. Imagine the organizational success that could be created if you decided that the fulfillment of every transaction or interaction would be your personal best. An experience at Crown Volvo reminds me of excellence.

My Volvo lease expired on a cold snowy day in February 2003 and one week after my daughter was born. I called the lease company to say I could not return the car on time, and I wanted to lease another Volvo. I was advised I would have to go to the dealership. I hung up and called the dealership with my story. The gentleman answering the phone took my lease requirements, asked me what color and style Volvo I was thinking about, and indicated he would come to our home with the paperwork. The next morning my doorbell rang, I was presented with paperwork for a new lease requiring only a signature. To my delight, a new blue Volvo was in my driveway. The salesman cleaned out my old Volvo, transferred the car seats between cars, and drove the old Volvo back to the dealership for lease return. He was intentional, he took control of the situation with humility, and he personally made it happen in 24 hours.

Make a mantra of being superior by focusing all attention on creating an excellent experience for customers, clients, and employees. Be excellent even during the small interactions like answering the telephone in the office or delivering a package. Excellence translates into revenue for your organization by leveraging intent, leadership, and personal accountability. There is reward and recognition for providing excellence in the form of enhanced personal brand, compensation increases, and career advancement.

Effort creates excellence.

• • •

27 Market Your Story

You have permission to speak for yourself. –Acts 26:1 (NIV). Paul spoke in front of a king to tell the story of his life, contributions, and values. *Let the redeemed of the Lord tell their story.* –Psalms 107:2 (NIV). When something good happens to you, no one can tell the story better than you.

The best marketing of skills, contributions, and aspirations is self-created. Relying on chance, a boss, or the human resources department is irresponsible. The good fortune of having significant accomplishments to talk about is a compelling reason to tell your story. Headlines are the banner or caption conveying key messages about you. Think about a newspaper headline that made you stop and read the article. Create the same response using a headline that is about you. For example: Mortgage Customers Ask for Mary Smith by Name to Get Fast and Accurate Answers.

It is customary to go to work in the office, put your head down, and dive into the details to get the job done. Accordingly, you expect decision makers to notice your hard work, value your contributions, and ensure you get to the next level. Unfortunately, hard work alone does not get the attention of an audience. Many times bosses, colleagues, clients, and customers need a reminder of the value your hard work produces. In other words, marketing continues throughout a career—market yourself to get the job, market to keep the job, and market to advance to the next level. Be the author of headlines and articles featuring personalized announcements of your talents and results. Be specific regarding projects generating revenue, budgets with no unfavorable variances, strategies effectively implemented, technology with 100% availability, hiring top talent, leader effectiveness, as well as positive community impact. Write one major headline annually for your professional development. Secondary headlines can be written more often—quarterly, monthly, or even weekly, depending on the pace of business. When you do not write a self-marketing message, decision makers may use incomplete, inaccurate, or stale information regarding your skills and contributions. Strike a balance between writing periodic headlines of meaningful accomplishments as opposed to self-promoting small contributions.

Start thinking and building your headline based on passion. What aspect of your career are you passionate about and want to do more? In other words, your story is a combination of what you do well and what you want others to know you like to do.

Create headlines to explain your character, contributions, and accomplishments. Having a marketing plan for internal and external headlines featuring your work will keep your name in circulation and create a buzz about your track record. Assess the audience to taper the content and forum for your headlines. As a rule, concise and factual are always best. For example an email to your boss on Friday afternoon with an invitation to contact you for more details might read as follows:

Subject (Headline): Monthly Sales Target Exceeded by 20%—Innovation, Hiring Model & Reduced Cost

- Created a web-based solution for out-of-stock merchandise, which gives the customer a real-time, alternate product with, free expedited shipping. (Passion)
- Designed a new sales team hiring profile to attract and recruit professionals with teaching backgrounds. Personally attended and interviewed during recruiting events.(Accelerator) Monthly employee retention trend improved 5% in last 90 days and customer satisfaction is 2% better.
- Exceeded budgeted sales growth by 20% while reducing unit cost due to productivity improvements and less returned merchandise. (Accomplishment)

Let me know if you want more details, I can be reached on my cell phone over the weekend.

The message in this email is timely and clear. Creating a series of these facts and accomplishments gets noticed. Get the information to the right person in the right format. This example used email but your boss may prefer a report with a highlight of the total column, a voicemail, or even a text message. Open the door for a one-on-one discussion about your accomplishments and ideas. This email will get a response. Be ready.

Equally important are proactive messages about aspirations. Timing is as important as the message. Talking about the next job before effectively contributing in the current role is not good. Talking about the next job at a social event with mixed company is not good. Talking about the next job during organizational change or turmoil is not good. When the timing is right, clues will exist throughout the organization—promotional announcements start to circulate, leadership development classes are offered, skip-level meetings take place, talent discussions become agenda items, special projects increase, leadership coaches are engaged, high potential employees get exposure to senior management, updates to development plans become required, and meetings to discuss your interests are scheduled. High potential and high performing employees are the first to be in a position to talk about career aspirations and should be prepared with an effective headline.

So how do you create a headline that identifies your aspirations? A high performing employee who is intellectually curious might say "I want to learn more about the inner workings of the business to be in a position to effectively make decisions about my career." A high performing employee with leadership potential might say "I would like to assume a role with increased levels of responsibility including developing people." A high performing leader who wants to contribute at the next level might say "I am interested in pursuing a career path that leads to a role as _____ (fill in the blank with a specific role when possible) in the organization."

Headlines regarding your career aspiration should evolve every two to three years as you move to the next level. My first major headline was accountant and auditor with strong project management and interpersonal skills. I used this headline to get my job at American Express in 1987. The second headline, outstanding performer with leadership potential. The third headline, effective leader with cross functional expertise. The fourth headline, high potential for 500+ staff leadership role in card operations. The fifth headline, proven people leader with potential to handle an increase in her job scope. The sixth headline, potential for executive leadership role with influence in the community as regional senior vice president. The seventh headline, seasoned executive leader announces transition outside the Company for personal reasons. My current headline is: dynamic businesswoman and public speaker, engaged community leader, and thoughtful author.

Headlines build resumes and resumes build careers.

• • •

28 Create A Plan

"Write this. Write what you see. Write it out in big block letters so that it can be read on the run. This vision-message is a witness pointing to what's coming. It aches for the coming—it can hardly wait! And it doesn't lie. If it seems slow in coming, wait. It's on its way. It will come right on time." –Habakkuk 2:2-3 (The Message). A written vision and plan become the proof of what can be expected in the future. The timing can be uncertain and requires patience.

A framework for how and when things will get done works well for career planning, project management, operations management, and even scheduling a calendar. Planning improves the likelihood of a successful completion by bringing order and structure to the implementation.

Staying with career planning as an example for our discussion, a career is the fulfillment of personal goals, aspirations, and opportunities—it is more than a job. Look forward to the next 5 years with a written plan that aligns career aspirations with personal and family goals. Self-guided career planning is one approach. It starts with a vision and a written plan. Good plans are informed with facts. Several professionals are unsure about the array of opportunities available.

As a step toward answering questions, learn about the economics of the industry in which you have an interest. This provides a view of the avenues for revenue generation and where investments are being made. These tangible data points allow you to evaluate how your skills and career choice might fit into a specific industry or company. I have five questions I often ask as I learn a new company or business process for career exploration and planning.

1. What are the major products and services offered and the supporting processes? (Production)
2. What are the various functional groups that support people in the organizations and are they considered core or support? (People)
3. How does the company leverage technology to support quality and delivery of products and services? (Systems)
4. How does the company make money? How does the company compare financially to peers in the industry? (Finance)
5. What is the customer lifecycle with the company? Are customers satisfied with products and services? (Customers and clients)

Career development is the next level of career planning. Development implies that the career has started, and it is now time to ensure it has a planned course toward enhancing skills and talents. Again, a vision and a documented plan are the first steps. There are six points to consider in career development. The plan must be specific (what skill do you want to develop); actionable (some specific task you can do to gain the skill), time sensitive (the task is doable in a specified period of time), about you (the majority of the tasks in the plan must be completed by you), linked to a vision (the plan must lead to a destination in your career), and measurable (the tasks must be recordable and quantifiable).

Planning and preparation to improve skills are never-ending during a career. Successful professionals are thinking one step ahead to ensure they have the right skills at the right time to meet the new demand. Complacency is the enemy of success.

A written plan turns a thought into reality.

• • •

29 Think

And we all, who with unveiled faces contemplate the Lord's glory, are being transformed into his image with ever-increasing glory, which comes from the Lord, who is the Spirit. –2 Corinthians 3:18 (NIV). We should free ourselves to reflect, study God's glory, and be changed because of what we learn.

Each hour of the day can be consumed by the activity of work. The more time you have the more work you can do. When should you stop working and just think? The desire to act can dominate thinking. Slowing down long enough to conceptualize the next new product, service, report, strategy, solution, new hire, career move, and revenue stream adds more value than ceaseless activity. Stop to think about what could be. Align yourself with futuristic thoughts and potential. Stand still long enough to let your spirituality and intellectual capacity speak to you. Being busy can inhibit growth.

Create a daily process to think about innovative solutions and ideas. Make a calendar entry for think-time or step away from the office for 30 minutes with a pad of paper. Most professionals might say they have think-time in the shower, driving in the car, and while eating alone. This is not true because in the shower you are distracted by washing, in the car you are distracted by driving, and at the table you are distracted by eating. Think-time is when the mind and body can be idle so that the Holy Spirit and brain can bring clarity and wonder.

Multi-tasking is a great and necessary thing for most. However, there are two occasions that I believe multi-tasking hurts our growth— when we pray and when we think. Prayer is a conversation with God. I pray to be in the presence of God to give thanks, ask for help, seek instructions, and I pray on behalf of others. As a separate act, I think to intellectually and logically act on the words of God and create a mental picture of what is possible. Some of my thinking is directed and other times, it jumps from subject to subject. In prayer, I have a two-way conversation. In think-time, it is a one-way conversation where I am silent. Forty thousand words for this book happened as a result of prayer and making time to think.

Stop reading and close your eyes for 15 minutes right now to deliberately think about what you want to accomplish or about something specific you need to do. Do this daily to think.

There was a time I would call my thinking—daydreaming. My thoughts seemed so far from reality and the realm of possible. That is until one day I began to act on the thoughts. My thoughts answer the "what if" questions. I think about data and how to perform an analysis and present the anticipated results. I think about what the presentation should look like and key messages to the audience. I think about what I would do or say if opportunity knocked on my door. Before becoming a senior vice president, I thought about what I would do to connect with the employees. I wrote those thoughts down and was able to go back and implement them. For example, I created the practice of greeting employees at the front door to say good morning and thank them for working at the company. I put forward a challenge to reward people who could recite the mission of the company. I created key messages for new hires regarding expectations. My thinking has become my advance planning for anticipated and the unexpected situations. Thinking is invaluable to my story and success.

Think as one of the best contributions you can make to your workday, career, and existence.

30 Focus on the Goal

The LORD will open the heavens, the storehouse of his bounty, to send rain on your land in season and to bless all the work of your hands. –Deuteronomy 28:12 (NIV). In pursuit of a goal, we encounter open doors and closed doors. Open doors are a blessing and result of God's grace. Closed doors can symbolize a pause, a detour, or a possible signal to go in another direction.

For those who experience a closed door on the road to achieve the vision, petition God for His will in your life, and once the vision is confirmed, take "no" as a strength builder. One closed door does not mean stop the vision, it might mean knock or take a detour to find an opened door someplace else. God purposefully closes doors in careers and lives. Some of those doors are sealed shut but we keep attempting to pry them open. Stop trying to pry open a closed door and seek clarification (petitioning God for His will in your life). Detours give strength to the vision as new information and increased determination are gathered on the journey. Validate questions and concerns to improve the vision. *So let's keep focused on that goal, those of us who want everything God has for us. If any of you have something else in mind, something less than total commitment, God will clear your blurred vision—you'll see it yet! Now that we're on the right track, let's stay on it.* –Philippians 3:15-16 (The Message).

Faith, courage, and perseverance keep the vision in sight. Life is full of miracles, open doors, closed doors, as well as detours. Be tenacious and undeterred to make the vision reality. *Where there is no vision, the people perish.* –Proverb 29:18 (NIV).

By God's grace, many open doors surfaced and I achieved my dream job with little resistance on the journey. It was part of the achievable plan for my life. My part of the plan was to pray, live Christian values, write the plan, and work toward achieving extraordinary performance whenever possible to fulfill the plan. High caliber performance and leadership competency turned into strong performance appraisals which translated into being promotable. My vision to reality took 10 years—not an overnight success.

At the start of the journey, I used my annual development plan as the method to get the goal in focus for me and my leader. I ensured the development also contained my strengths as action items. People leadership and strategic thinking were the two items on my plan. I had sizable people leadership within project management and leading without authority. However, I needed more experience leading a team of direct reports with diverse backgrounds. Putting it on my development plan put it in front of my bosses as a request for a team and then a larger team. It was a successful approach to get increasing levels of people responsibility.

My second development plan goal item was—strategic thinking, innovative and creative ideas that lead to new products, services, and solutions. My goal was to become a methodical thinker on the subjects of business growth and process improvements. Putting strategic thinking on a plan and finding the right projects to learn this skill, got me to the goal. The goal took many years to accomplish. I was known as a strong implementation person. Accordingly, I spent more time getting projects to the finish line than strategically thinking about new projects. Finally, the big breaks started to come in a natural sequence of understanding the business, strong people leadership, and analytical skills which all linked to strategic thinking.

Whether your vision and goal is to get a job, keep a job, advance in a job, avoid foreclosure on a home, or start a business, the end point is attainable if you are willing to persevere. Again, write the vision and be prepared for open and closed doors. *For everyone who asks receives; the one who seeks finds; and to the one who knocks, the door will be opened.* –Matthew 7:8 (NIV). What are the one or two things you need to focus on to bring your performance to *The Next Level?*

Focus on the goal to benefit from the lessons behind open and closed doors.

• • •

31 Communicate

Seek first to understand, then to be understood. –Proverbs 18:13 (NIV).
*And don't say anything you don't mean. This counsel is embedded deep
in your traditions. You only make things worse when you lay down a
smoke screen of pious talk saying I'll pray for you and never doing it
or saying God be with you and not meaning it. You don't make your
words true by embellishing them with religious lace. In making your
speech sound more religious, it becomes less true. Just say yes and
no. When you manipulate words to get your own way, you go wrong.*
–Matthew 5:37 (The Message). Communication is the single means
of delivering a message to create an understanding between two
or more parties.

The elements of understandable communication are: **intent, content
and form**. Careers get off to great starts because of the merit of
communication during the interview (e.g. the candidate presents
outstanding credentials valued by the interviewer). Likewise, careers
end because of poor communication and omission (e.g. sexual
harassment statements to create fear or not telling a leader about a
significant business issue). To move to the next level, the elements of
intent, content, and form must work in concert with a set of business
expectations. People value what they understand.

Communicate: **Intent**

Communicators have intent for every message delivered. As such, the objective of a message is either constructive or destructive. In business, positive and negative messages are necessary. The problem comes at the extremes in either direction which can be counterproductive. Too nice—may impede the growth of an organization; people waste resources by allowing ineffective projects to continue for the sake of not hurting someone's feelings. Mean-spirited communications have a personal impact that paralyzes people with anger.

Successful organizations encourage and develop training for communication to ensure employees assemble effective presentations and relay reliable messages. The constructive intent and purpose(s) for communication has to be established first.

Conversations with a single intent are the most effective. Trying to inform, confront, and give feedback in a single interaction is difficult for even the most seasoned communicators. Effective communication is about understanding. Once the primary intent is established, take time to have a full conversation that allows all parties to participate and end with everyone having the same understanding.

Organize conversations to: state the objective, stay on topic, and summarize the conversation. Conversations with a specific intent have a planned result.

One intent of a conversation might be to confront which is a communication technique professionals struggle to execute. The ability to confront a situation and come to an agreement on how to reverse negative performance is a good thing for all parties involved. Constructive confrontation has a positive intent to bring forward evidence on why a situation must and should change. The message is firm and civil.

Example A: Michael, we have an emergency in the office. The system upgrade that went into effect last night has resulted in missing client information. We just emailed you examples of missing name and balance information. Please get the technology team to review the examples, and find a fix by the time the staff begins taking client call in the next 30 minutes. Let's do a root cause analysis immediately after the fix goes in to see what went wrong and in the meantime, stop any further planned system changes until we talk. Example B: Michael what did your team do to the system? Client information is missing. Please get the idiot that did not test the code for quality control to back out the system change before our clients and service people find out. I want an explanation before some heads roll.

Both examples relay a sense of urgency. The first statement gives an understanding of the issue and why and when it must change. The second gives the same information but is overshadowed by a hostile and destructive tone leaving Michael feeling attacked, defeated, and on the defense. Going into a conversation with the intent to be destructive never yields a positive outcome. It is acceptable to be angry at work and to let people know you are angry but your word choice must be focused on the issue, not the person. How we communicate during an error is as important as fixing the error. Character attributes such as compassion, curiosity, and integrity compliment effective communication.

Communicate: **Content**

Content is the accumulation of words (and some body language) to convey a message. The audience has the prerogative to agree or disagree with any or all of the content presented. The content of a communication may be fact or opinion but it must be appropriate and understandable.

The right words set the tone for understanding but the wrong choice of words can confuse or reduce understanding. Audience-oriented content works best. Selecting the right words for the audience to understand a message is not automatic and needs preparation and practice. Great orators write their messages and use a practice audience to validate the effectiveness of the content. One wrong word could make the impact null and void. *Reckless words pierce like a sword, but the tongue of the wise brings healing.* —Proverbs 12:18 (NIV). To be effective at creating communications that are understandable, the content and tone must be aligned. Sharing business results that need improvement (content) must give immediate solutions (urgent tone) to reverse the trend. Your personal style drives the tone and determines the use of a single or multiple tones.

Developing the content for communication needs an element of flexibility because each member of an audience understands and learns differently. What works in one environment may not work in another. An effective communicator has sensors to determine if the audience got it or missed it. Sensors include observation of body language queues from the audience, requests for in-the-moment feedback, and audible reactions. What facial expression do you exhibit when you do not understand? Do you squint? Is your mouth open, or both?

Adjust content that does not create understanding. Get feedback to improve the content of your message.

The style and content of my written communication differs from what I will present in front of a physical audience. My written communication in memos, email, text, letters, and presentation is more formal and traditional. When making a public presentation to an audience, I tend to use humor and personal stories to create understanding and engagement. Depending on the audience, I will infuse pop culture for relevance. Throughout my career, I have used tone to set the stage. Tough messages about business performance brought out urgency, empathy, and inspiration. Celebratory messages have included drama, pop culture, and jokes.

The exact words matched to the right tone will relay a clear and compelling message to ensure the same understanding is reached by the audience. Are people responding to your messages as you would expect?

Communicate: **Form**

Make the most of every opportunity. Be gracious in your speech. The goal is to bring out the best in others in a conversation, not put them down, and not cut them out. –Colossians 4:6 (The Message). The format for communication is dependent on intent and content. Determine the substance before form. Reliable communication aligns verbal and nonverbal forms. Nodding yes and saying no are simple examples of mixed and unreliable communication.

Verbal communication (to see or hear a message) has an expanding medium—from person to person, and extends beyond traditional print (presentations, books and magazines) to include television, video conference, email, text, sign language, social media, and instant messaging. Nonverbal communication is contained in physical gestures, listening, and silence.

Verbal communication contributes to the effectiveness of the message. Speaking face-to-face is best for conveying negative messages. Reward and recognition has more flexibility but should be personalized. Using the wrong format can have numerous outcomes. Terminations via email generate ill-will. Feedback regarding performance that needs improvement during a conference call violates trust. Announcing company closings on Facebook can cause chaos or be legally problematic. Promotion announcements during national conferences are inspiring but sharing the new salary violates personnel privacy constraints. You get the point.

The workplace is global and adjusting expectations makes it easier to conduct business. Some formats enable speed and efficiency while reducing complexity. Performance appraisal discussions via telephone with an email copy are becoming perfectly acceptable at all levels. In addition, terminations are happening via telephone every day because of logistics. New assignments are coming via webinar. Meeting requests are sent via text messages. Good judgment is the best decision maker to determine the most effective form(s) for written and verbal communication.

Nonverbal communication is demonstrated through conscious or unconscious gestures, movements, and stillness. Nonverbal communication is interpreted by the recipient before the first word is spoken and lingers long after the last word is spoken. The book of Job tells a story that includes nonverbal communication through body language and silence as factors of his successful influence. *"Men and women listened when I spoke, hung expectantly on my every word. After I spoke, they'd be quiet, taking it all in. They welcomed my counsel like spring rain, drinking it all in. When I smiled at them, they could hardly believe it; their faces lit up, their troubles took wing! I was their leader, establishing the mood and setting the pace by which they lived. Where I led, they followed."* –Job 29:21-25 (The Message).

Job combined words and body language to influence. The energy of his smile provided a positive atmosphere. How many ways can we communicate without using words? Three ways are—body language, listening, and silence.

He who answers before listening—that is his folly and his shame. –Proverbs 18:13 (NIV). Listening first helps to gain an understanding. The reputation of being a strong listener is admired and trusted. A great talker who does not listen can translate into hot air and nonsense. A young man once told me, we have two ears and one mouth for a reason. Effective communication happens when active listening takes place. We rarely remember the best listener during a meeting. However, the listener often makes great progress after the meeting when compared to the verbose communicator in the meeting.

There is a time for everything, and a season for every activity under the heavens: a time to be silent and a time to speak. –Ecclesiastes 3:1 and 7 (NIV). God has a plan, and our words can disrupt or slow down the plan. Exercise good judgment and have a purpose when speaking and when being silent. Silence is the intention not to say a word even when solicited for a comment. Silence is an answer, but it is also subjective. The interpretation might not be the answer you want to give.

Silence is a good offensive position in adversity. Good silence is not responding when being criticized by your boss in a meeting of your peers. *Those who guard their mouths and their tongues keep themselves from calamity.* –Proverbs 21:22 (NIV). The wisdom to recognize a losing battle when conflict arises avoids a negative confrontation. On the other hand, silence can cause damage to a career. Bad silence has no input in the weekly staff meeting while others provide updates and share new ideas. Fear can be gripping and cause silence. Not speaking up in a collaborative business environment devalues your presence. Have the courage to share your thoughts or ask clarifying questions to demonstrate understanding and engagement.

Communicate to be understood because people value what they understand.

• • •

32 Ask for Help

*Do not be anxious about anything, but in everything, by prayer and petition, with thanksgiving, present your requests to God. And the peace of God, which transcends all understanding, will guard your hearts and your minds in Christ Jesus. –*Philippians 4:6-7 (NIV). *This is the confidence we have in approaching God: that if we ask anything according to his will, he hears us. And if we know that he hears us–whatever we ask—we know that we have what we asked of Him. –*1 John 5:14-15 (NIV). God expects us to ask for His help.

Asking for help to launch a career or business endeavor is a winning proposition. The questions then are: whom do you ask for help and in what area do you ask for help? God is a good start for all of our requests. *You do not have because you do not ask God. –*James 4:2 (NIV).

Second, ask for help from sources that have the information you need. The 21st century offers personal assistance in a nanosecond through online search tools, social media, smart phones, GPS, and several other choices. Yet, some requests are not answered through technology. A personal interaction based on a relationship is a common avenue for support, advice, and coaching in business. Is it smart to ask for help, or is figuring it out on your own a better way to learn? The answer is both. Seek assistance when that answer lies outside your area of expertise. Different skills are disbursed to different people so that we can depend on each other for our needs. *There are different kinds of gifts, but the same Spirit. There are different kinds of service, but the same Lord. There are different kinds of working, but the same God works all of them in all men. Now to each one the manifestation of the Spirit is given for the common good.* –1 Corinthians 12:4-7 (NIV).

Ask for help from the right source and ask for something specific within a specific timeline. Seeking assistance is part of the design of good careers and good business. Getting help diversifies the influence on a situation and provides an outside perspective. Help takes on all forms including: consultants, leaders, regulatory agencies, coaches, peers, competitors, cross-functional teams, community leaders, focus groups, auditors, friends, family, and religious leaders.

The goal of getting it done the smartest way possible leads many professionals to seek assistance. On-the-job training starts the process of asking for help. My track record has been greatly influenced by the expertise of others. Getting assistance and knowledge from others has allowed me to know enough to be conversational about a topic. In other cases, I have become an expert because of the knowledge sharing from a consultant or colleague. It is smart to ask for help and is an efficient use of company resources. The inquiry has to be specific and addressed to a resource that has the most relevant knowledge. Otherwise, you get extraneous information. Timing matters—be specific, share time constraints, and set expectations for deliverables.

I took a job as vice president of operations without direct training in operations management. I had general knowledge but not enough to advance the performance of all aspects of the group. I asked a million questions every day but that was not enough. I needed help. The main hub of the operations was "the desk." I made a plan to begin and end my day by going to the desk and asking employees to teach me how to manage call flow and resources. The lessons were many and complicated. I spent hours at the desk including evenings and weekends. These front-line employees were extraordinary and knew the ins and outs. I was getting help from the desk but I needed more help. I then asked an engineer who was responsible for forecasting and planning to help me understand predicting call distributions and resource efficiencies. I had help because I asked for help to help me do my job. After approximately 60 days of help, it clicked and I understood the input, output, and measures of success. I was the vice president but I needed the help of people who reported to me. I was not too proud to ask for help. Together we had tremendous respect for one another which made it a beneficial relationship. Are you sitting at your desk in need of help but too proud to ask? Do you offer to help others who could benefit from your knowledge?

Asking for help is smart, resourceful, and effective.

• • •

33 Increase Knowledge

Not until halfway through the Feast did Jesus go up to the temple courts and begin to teach. The Jews were amazed and asked, "How did this man get such learning without having studied?" Jesus answered, "My teaching is not my own. It comes from him who sent me. –John 7:14-16 (NIV). Listen, my sons, to a father's instruction; pay attention and gain understanding. I give you sound learning, so do not forsake my teaching. –Proverbs 4:1-2 (NIV). Instruct a wise man and he will be wiser still; teach a righteous man and he will add to his learning. –Proverbs 9:9 (NIV). To learn, to study, and to teach are fundamental aspects of ministry and bring us closer to God.

The willingness to learn new things and apply the knowledge is a predictor of long-term success and leadership potential. The brain is a living organ that requires stimulation and information. To close off the brain from practical and intellectual experiences stops life and a career in its tracks. Spend time reading, researching, and experimenting to prolong learning.

Mainstream and industry periodicals, town hall meetings, coaching sessions, and continuing professional education represent a short list of resources to keep you abreast of relevant trends while offering you new skills to apply in the workplace. God expects us to get wisdom and understanding beyond our present levels of intelligence about His word and life on earth. *The beginning of wisdom is this: Get wisdom. Though it cost all you have, get understanding.* –Proverbs 4:7 (NIV). What new information, work techniques, or insight have you acquired over the last 30 days? No matter how much of an expert you are, there is always room to enhance your core skills or leadership competency.

Learning should concentrate on the long-term value. The financial cost of skill and career development is tuition we must pay for career success. Make a mission to learn about processes related to your job. Knowing a little about everything avoids the risk of totaling relying on the knowledge and skills of others. The goal is not to be overwhelmed by too much information but to be comfortable that you know enough to ensure the process is headed in the right direction.

My intellectual curiosity ensures that I ask questions to gather relevant knowledge about areas that impact my work or are of personal interest. The questions include: what position the organization would like to be in ten years from now? How does strategy impact current or future customers? Are people or communities hurt by the future direction of the organization? Who are the direct and indirect competitors? Is the workforce diverse and stable? Are customers and clients satisfied with the products and services? What are the corporate and community challenges and strengths?

My best learning is hands-on experience. I trust everybody but I need to see and touch it for myself to increase my knowledge. As a result of learning new business disciplines, I could move from audit and accounting into risk management and from risk management into operations management. The core connection between the areas of my career was based on analytical skills and the willingness to learn. My training exposed me to different regulatory and compliance rules, use of multiple technological interfaces, process and procedural details, and a global network of people.

My transition from internal audit to risk management meant I needed to acquire a new set of skills. I sat next to colleagues in my group who did quantitative analysis by using computer programs to extract data, isolate the important numbers, and then determine the relationships and story of the data to address a problem. I had no natural interest in the mechanics of data extraction to perform an analysis. However, it was important for me to understand the process to be successful in my new role. So I asked a million questions and eventually learned enough to do my job. I increased my knowledge but did not gain expert status. I was able to gain ,credibility and consult with people who were proficient as computer programmers and statisticians. Our partnership led to success working on cross-functional teams where we spoke the same language and could review the analysis together to draw conclusions. I was grateful not to be on the sideline when discussions were underway about data analysis. I reciprocated by sharing my knowledge of financial analysis, operating procedures, regulatory guidelines, and people leadership.

How do you satisfy your curiosity to gain knowledge? Have you taken advantage of opportunities to learn a new job function? Could increasing your knowledge offer you more control of your life with expanded career options? What knowledge or learning experience would enrich your life?

Lifelong learning increases your relevance and opportunities.

• • •

34 Do More

As for other matters, brothers and sisters, we instructed you how to live in order to please God, as in fact you are living. Now we ask you and urge you in the Lord Jesus to do this more and more. –1 Thessalonians 4:1 (NIV). *And in fact, you do love all of God's family throughout Macedonia. Yet we urge you, brothers and sisters, to do so more and more.* –1 Thessalonians 4:10 (NIV). God expects that if you do His will and follow His word, you will not stop but seek after Him more.

People and organizations ranking as top performers are expected to do more to stay on top—with more innovation, more products, and more services. Last year's contributions have little to do with measuring value in the current year. When you do something good, people come to expect that you will continue to do more good things. The underlying question is what have you done lately?

In lean years of economic downturns, financial recovery, or reengineering, you will be asked to do more with less. That is to increase productivity with fewer resources than in prior years. As a general rule, look to optimize your performance by prioritizing resources to maximize output. The two dominant line items on a financial statement that grab the attention of leadership are total revenue (contributions, sales, donations, income, etc) and total expenses. When you are looking to do more to help the organization achieve its goals, look to those two lines first. How can you do more to increase income and decrease expenses while benefiting all constituents? Regardless of the mission of your organization, dollars and cents matter. The astute professional will bring good ideas forward in conjunction with the financial benefits and implications. They see the opportunity for the firm to enhance relationship management which has a cost benefit. Call customers to address complaints instead of sending a letter or email. While in conversation, solve the problem and determine their overall satisfaction. Determine if there are loyalty, upgrade, or new products and services to offer the customer.

The notion of doing more must be internalized before it becomes an outward business behavior. Doing more is stretching you beyond previous accomplishments—reshape, transform, breakthrough, quantum leaps, improved inventions, out of the box. Examples of more include rethinking your production process to increase targets to a new level, taking on new tasks on a project team, and engaging in strategic planning by putting progressive ideas on the table. More can also include lending your corporate experience to help the church market the pre-school to increase enrollment. In return, someone might lend you a skill to help achieve your corporate goals. In a community association, more could mean starting evening citizen town hall meetings to educate on the latest local government and housing trends. This could lead to more volunteer resources for problem solving. Whining about the need for more resources before you can do more (at work, in the community, or at home) is a circular discussion. Instead, start the trend of doing more in order to attract more resources to your cause. A guaranteed rate of return makes it easy to invest in your work. Are you waiting for more resources before you attempt to do more?

Creativity and innovation are sometimes required to do more with existing resources. In one of the small groups I was responsible for managing, an employee suggested that we capture more opportunities to say yes to customers. He realized that our process was not designed to handle transactions that required multiple interactions with vendors. It was a missed opportunity to capture more revenue. This employee took it upon himself to follow transactions through the multiple stages and provide the necessary approvals. His process was manual but once he brought it to my attention, we started to design an automated solution. The revenue benefit was not significant enough to get strategic investment dollars but it was the right thing to do. We accomplished as much automation as we could with no incremental investments. We did get it off the ground and were able to later justify some investment dollars based on our revenue contributions and value creation for customers. The courage of one employee to do more out of concern for customers and vendors caused a shift in how we did business. Do you think about what you could do to make improvements to address customer complaints? Would you continue to make suggestions for improvement when investment dollars are not available?

Do more before asking for more.

• • •

35 Resolve Conflict

A man's wisdom gives him patience; it is to his glory to overlook an offense. –Proverbs 19:11 (NIV). *"If your brother sins against you go and show him his fault, just between the two of you. If he listens to you, you have won your brother over. But if he will not listen, take one or two others along, so that 'every matter may be established by the testimony of two or three witnesses.'*–Matthew 18:15-16 (NIV). *For though we live in the world, we do not wage war as the world does.* –2 Corinthians 10:3 (NIV). *The strong forgive.* –Matthew 6:14 (NIV). God sets an infallible standard for conflict resolution which relies on love, strength, and forgiveness.

Undoubtedly, business interactions will result in tension on one occasion or another. These tense moments should not be taken personally—it's just business. Colleagues in business often step out of line and offend others. The created tension is legitimate and may stem from abusive language, manipulation, suspicions, bias, false accusations, harassment, disagreements, disrespect, or being overlooked. These conflicts can destroy work relationships, organizational progress, business reputations, workplace dynamics, and careers. Some conflicts have been known to extend outside the office. Most people can pinpoint at least one hostile relationship in the workplace and its unhealthy effect. Still, professionals allow conflict to permeate the environment. Human nature is competitive and arrogant and when not controlled can lead to conflicts between professionals.

The solution to conflict includes forgiveness. It is impossible to work through a conflict unless the parties are willing to set aside the behavior or occurrence, forgive, and then move forward to achieve common goals. Unfortunately, counterproductive to moving forward, people would rather analyze the conflict, endlessly talk about the conflict, bring others into the conflict, and hold onto the conflict. The analysis, discussion, convening, and the grip of conflict can kill the spirit of people and the culture of a company. Some relationships are so tarnished that the original cause of the conflict is no longer recallable. People are content and fixed in anger. *Do not repay evil with evil or insult with insult. On the contrary, repay evil with blessing, because to this you were called so that you may inherit a blessing.* –1 Peter 3:7-9 (NIV). The weak never forget, never forgive, and never have peace. Unresolved conflict keeps people tied to the past. *Get rid of all bitterness, rage and anger, brawling and slander, along with every form of malice. Be kind and compassionate to one another, forgiving each other, just as in Christ God forgave you.* –Ephesians 4:32 (NIV).Why are you in conflict with a colleague?

Being tolerant can help us move toward forgiveness. In turn, forgiveness allows everyone to move forward. Address the root cause of a conflict you have with others through patience, kindness, and the facts. In constructive conflict and resolution, we can grow and change for the better.

Get freedom from the stress of workplace conflicts by intentionally resolving issues as they arise. Ninety-nine percent of my work-related conflicts were resolved because I was willing to take the first step. Forgiving benefited me most because it stopped the emotional chaos of conflict. Second, forgiveness released the other person from a negative connection with me. When something goes wrong, goes against the grain, or goes against the plan, I retreat away from the heat of the situation. The retreat is a time for cooling off and getting perspective. Conflict is only resolved if it is addressed with a calm head. *Bear with each other and forgive one another if any of you has a grievance against someone. Forgive as the Lord forgave you.* –Colossians 3:13 (NIV). After the retreat, I initiate a discussion. The receiver can be accepting or resisting. Regardless of how the other person might respond, I remain focused and complete my objective of getting the facts on the table, listening to all parties, stating my forgiveness, and offering solutions to move forward. Admittedly, I have not always retreated and used the draft button in an email. I have regretted every email sent in anger as a result of a conflict. I ignored the voice that said "don't hit that send button". These messages were usually factual, but the tone was inappropriate and unforgiving. Subsequently, I have had to readdress the conflict by retracting the email and resolving the issue with a calm head. As you might imagine, too much time can be spent addressing a conflict if it is done with a hot head versus a cool head.

Resolve conflicts through forgiveness and make the choice to move forward.

• • •

36 Gather Data

Believe me when I say that I am in the Father and the Father is in me; or at least believe on the evidence of the works themselves. –John 14:11(NIV). If it was torn to pieces by a wild animal, the neighbor shall bring in the remains as evidence and shall not be required to pay for the torn animal. –Exodus 22:13 (NIV). God is willing to give us proof of his glorious power and superiority.

Prepared professionals present their case with facts to support action plan recommendations, funding requests, and feedback discussions. Reasonable people do not have blind trust in the words of others. God provides examples of His power throughout the Bible so that we have evidence of His sovereignty. Smart professionals exercise curiosity and discernment by asking questions and examining data to support a topic. Intellectual curiosity sets the expectation that evidence-based discussions and decisions will take place. The data can be qualitative or quantitative. The accuracy and sustainability of decisions is greatly increased when it is based on supporting data.

There is a real caution concerning gathering evidence or proof to support a cause—overwhelmed by information. The pitfall of over analyzing information is it slows the decision-making process. The combination of art and science can yield effective outcomes. Wit, gut-feeling, experience, tribal knowledge, and personal opinion play a role with concrete data to draw conclusions.

My credibility is largely based on knowledge extracted from experience and data. I lean heavily on research before forming an opinion. The Internet is a powerful tool for instant information. There is no excuse for not having data to support opinions and decisions. In my career at American Express, the culture required quantitative evidence. Augmenting the evidence with common sense became a sustaining factor in my leadership effectiveness. A core person on every team I create is an analytical resource—to extract, analyze, and report usable information. Many protracted discussions can be shortened by introducing useful data points to keep the conversation focused and factual. It can be frustrating to be engaged in a circular discussion based on the opinions of a few. It is always helpful to substantiate an opinion with evidence to get buy-in, educate, or redirect. The most favorable outcome of being evidence-based is that new people get educated with the data which increases the levels of institutional knowledge and informed decision making.

I was working with my team on rewriting collection letters. The goal was to improve the effectiveness of communication to customers as measured by the customer making a payment on a past due account. We could have gotten two people in a room and professed to be good writers and written the letters. Instead, we gathered competitive intelligence about what other companies across different industries were writing to customers to prompt a payment. A simple part of this data gathering was asking everyone in the department to get competitor letters from the mail of friends and family to share with the project team. Additionally, we held focus groups with customers to determine which letter would cause them to take action by making a payment. Gathering this collection of data points greatly improved the final output of the letter rewrite. We wrote letters that customers actually understood. Imagine the power of being informed by data.

Put the facts on the table so that people are well informed about why a decision has been made. Likewise, ask for the facts if they are not offered. Many people make bad decisions because they do not ask questions or ask for proof.

Be guided by God and the fact-based evidence you gather.

• • •

37 Collaborate

Any kingdom divided against itself will be ruined, and a house divided against itself will fall. –Luke 11:17 (NIV). Spiritual unity and working collaboratively strengthens the church and its people.

Organizations achieve greater levels of marketplace leadership with a collaborative employee base. Colleagues sharing ideas and rooting for the success of the team can deliver record-breaking profits within an industry. Professionals who collaborate will ensure that the plan and goals are clear to each member of the team. The team has a visible and philosophical unity. What brand stands out in your mind when you think about a popular computer or cell phone? When you walk into the retail outlet of that brand, do the employees behave in a collaborative method between the greeters, sales, and technical staff? Is it a seamless transition? Team members that connect the dots between their specific roles and the expertise of others understand the need to cooperate. In a row boat, everyone must pull the oars in the same direction. Otherwise, the boat will not move forward and could potentially turn over, dumping everyone into the water.

Division in leadership ranks or between management and the front line workers creates a distraction that takes the focus away from high quality products and services. The friction of infighting will waste time, become a newspaper headline, cause resignations and terminations, and ultimately result in lost revenue for the company.

Do you and do your colleagues willingly collaborate with others? Collaboration is binary, either you collaborate or you do not. When collaboration is impossible between a team and leader or individual team members, someone must be removed from the equation. The unity of an organization is more important than any one person. Collaboration puts all ideas on the table for discussion and exploration. However, once a decision is made, every person is asked to follow the approved plan, approach, and process. If your counterargument, opinion, or evidence is not incorporated into the final decision, get over it. If you cannot get over it, quit. Do not stay in a job to create discord or continually refuse to follow the approved plan of action. The leader who identifies a lack of collaboration in the organization becomes more effective and respected if the issue is addressed. In addressing the unwillingness to cooperate among the employee populations, find out why people do not collaborate, answer all open questions, and offer solutions. Ultimately, a leader must ensure the mission for the work is transparent and everyone is on board. When the employee base cannot be unified to do the work, offer an off-ramp to uncooperative people. The exit strategy may vary, but the goal is always to quickly get uncooperative people off the team.

In my experience, collaboration is non-negotiable. Collaboration is 100% controllable by an individual. I am willing to work with anybody and everybody. I expect the same from others. Unity can get the job done correctly in the least amount of time. Smart people do not always agree on a single ideology. Instead, they agree to disagree and then move on by working together. I willingly try other ideas as the solution because the team selected an alternative answer. Solving the problem should outweigh any single opinion or ego. Mutual respect among team members creates an environment for collaboration. My fellow board of directors members share a passion for the organization's mission. At work I rely on high quality professionals and a transparent decision-making process as key elements in a collaborative culture.

My most interesting cross-functional project was formed to determine what fee to charge customers. There was great debate of competitive analysis, internal analysis on future spending, potential customer cancellation rates, and revenue projections. Nobody fully agreed with another person. We collaborated on what information was required to make a decision. Being satisfied we had the necessary information, we pushed our way through the data, customer feedback, financials, marketplace trends, and internal viewpoints. We agreed on a number after several discussions. The decision was made and the next step was implementation. We fully united behind the decision.

Collaborate for the sake of unity to ensure the best results.

• • •

38 Follow Protocol

Everything should be done in a fitting and orderly way. –1 Corinthians 14:40 (NIV). *Let all things be done decently and in order.* –1 Corinthians 14:40 (KJV). Paul instructs us, and God wants our actions to be respectful and considerate to others. In addition, the appropriateness of our actions brings credibility.

The protocol within a business is designed to support the culture and mission of the company. Protocol is the interpretation of policy, procedures, etiquette, training, and standards. Following the protocol in your organization can keep you out of trouble. The rules of business protocol can be simple, elusive, written, or unwritten. God provides a basic framework for how to get things done at work and in life. The Bible links decency and order—what we do and how we do it.

Are your workplace actions decent and in order? Before you answer, put aside your personal interests and desires. The protocol is not about you. Learning the rules of engagement can start with observing what is done by others, and listening to what is said by others. Watch, listen, then read the code of conduct, training manuals, and other materials to learn the written and implied rules. Watch, listen, read the rules, and then ask questions to get clarity on what to do and how to take action. Watch, listen, read the rules, ask questions, and then act with openness to embrace feedback. The feedback can include endorsement or redirection of your actions. Feedback is a gift that gets you on the right track. Just like setting a table, there is a protocol. We only get a few opportunities to demonstrate proficiency with protocol. The level of rigidity differs between companies and people but, when in doubt—ask. Organizations have written protocols for the major areas such as: system changes, approval authority, research standards, and product development. Some unwritten protocols might include seating in meetings, formats for presentations, attendee lists for meetings, filing an internal complaint, and what not to wear to work.

My learning curve from organization to organization is usually short regarding the protocol and has the benefit of no career-ending mistakes in 29 years. My simple framework to navigating most protocol is: watch, listen, read to learn the rules, ask questions, and act with flexibility. Being new on a job and a new member on the board of directors offers two options—add no value because I don't know the protocol or immediately contribute because I quickly learn the protocol. Doing things decently and in order sets a standard for what others can expect regarding my contributions. In December 1987 and 60 days into a new job, I was in a meeting in Englewood, Colorado when a senior vice president challenged my presentation. The discussion became tense, and the leader became aggressive. My natural instinct was to defend my presentation. Although my facts were correct, I did not show respect for the chain of command. I was reprimanded for my tone, defensive posture, and not deferring to my boss. *"Everything is permissible"—but not everything is beneficial. "Everything is permissible"—but not everything is constructive.* −1 Corinthians 10:23 (NIV).

That business trip was a moment of truth which caused me to question how I could have done things differently. I learned to be cognizant of the chain of command and find more professional channels to address the negative treatment I received from others. This meant I had to be more disciplined and courageous by maintaining my professional behavior. Although the work I presented was accurate, it was not the most important consideration for my career. I had to step back and assess being right as compared to being well regarded and respected. In the years since 1987, I have demonstrated the decorum of being right, respectful, and gracious.

Follow protocol—written and unwritten—to make impressions and statements about your professional maturity and wisdom.

• • •

39 Make A Decision

If any of you lacks wisdom, you should ask God, who gives generously to all without finding fault, and it will be given to you. But when you ask, you must believe and not doubt, because the one who doubts is like a wave of the sea, blown and tossed by the wind. –James 1:5-6 (NIV). *The heart of the discerning acquires knowledge, for the ears of the wise seek it out.* –Proverbs 18:15 (NIV). *Trust in the LORD with all your heart and lean not on your own understanding; in all your ways submit to him, and he will make your paths straight.* –Proverbs 3:5-6 (NIV). The Lord provides incremental wisdom and knowledge to assist with decision making.

Decision making is in the scope of all roles in an organization. Little formal training is offered to address the challenges of decision making. Professionals are expected to use good judgment, relevant data, and expertise to come to the right conclusion. Decision points can represent a fork in the road or a stop sign. In either case, one decision might be the reason for a project to succeed or fail. The unknown impact of a decision and the uncertainty of what can happen can breed fear and lead to no decision being made. Personally, I make decisions and move on. With bigger issues, I pray, do research, and likewise make the choice and move on. I revisit very few decisions, and I usually avoid second guessing a decision.

Indecision is a decision to be unreliable. Indecision will cause the people in the organization to become frustrated and unproductive. There is no single right answer for how to make decisions. Three pertinent principles include a consistent decision-making philosophy, use of all available resources (people and data) without being subject to analysis paralysis, and communication of the decision in a timely manner. Correcting a decision is equally as important as making the original decision. Have the courage to reverse a decision if you find out the original decision was wrong.

A new quality control measurement process needed to be put into place based on analysis of errors being made by employees. The team needed to decide how many allowable errors a person could make before being subject to termination. We wanted to be fair but fair can never be fair to everyone. We made a decision, communicated the new standard, trained everyone, put in daily reporting, and call monitoring playback. Quickly names started to emerge for termination due to excessive quality errors. The decision was made, and the terminations had to happen given the business risk of errors. In the end, quality dramatically improved.

Being decisive with a high degree of accuracy and speed are important considerations for my decision making. Getting the decision right benefits all parties concerned, while speed keeps everyone productive. Whether it was in the office, in the community, or at home, I find it of extreme importance to get answers to people who need a decision. Additionally, I am willing to be transparent by explaining how I arrive at a specific decision and the impact to all constituents.

In a service center, we had to decide the work schedules for hundreds of employees. When customers call, you want to ensure someone is available to answer the call. Do we undergo a process to change the schedules of employees twice in a year? Should management upset the lives of everyone so the business can answer almost 95% of the calls from customers within seconds? Is there a less intrusive way to manage customer and employee expectations? Is it reasonable to change a person's work schedule every two years? Is a work schedule decision a human consideration or a business benefit? How do people operate their personal lives without a fixed work schedule? Do people quit when management decisions do not take into account the human factor? What is the cost of replacing an employee compared to some potential inefficiency in a work week?

There can be a list of questions when it is time to make a decision. My goal would be to make a decision that benefits both customers and employees whenever possible. Massive change to an employee's work schedule in this example has human considerations and is not exclusively a paper and data decision. Early in my operations management career, I transitioned from annual work schedule changes for collections representatives to a more continuance process based on a combination of employee requests and customers needs—a win win. In addition, we added in a factor to prioritize who received the best schedules or their first choice based on performance (value) and not tenure. Sometimes the decision needed is more than the direct question in front of you. When a decision is needed, consider the lateral and downstream impact of the decision. Making one decision could prove to be a benefit for indirect processes and people. In this case, stopping the annual and sometimes twice a year mass employee work schedule change in exchange for a performance-based work schedule change request directly benefited customers and high performing employees.

As a board of directors member, when the committee I am on makes a decision, I ensure the background is shared to ensure the basis for the decision is transparent. In an economic downturn with decreasing charitable contributions, do you give raises to employees in not-for-profit industries? Why and why not? What are the optics of a decision? How do you leverage data and good judgment to support a decision?

How do you respond when people disagree with the communicated decision?

Selling an unpopular decision can open up a new discussion and hostility. Everyone will not agree with every decision you make. It is important to go back to transparency. How did you make the decision? How does the decision benefit the business? How does the decision benefit or not benefit employees? Can employees look at the data used in decision making? Is the decision permanent? Once all the sharable information is provided, it is important to end the debate. Some people start the debate after the decision is made. Be compassionate and allow people the opportunity to give feedback without consequences. After listening and responding to the feedback, ask people to go back to work.

Make a decision to create the direction.

• • •

40 Take Risks

"It's also like a man going off on an extended trip. He called his servants together and delegated responsibilities. To one he gave five thousand dollars, to another two thousand, to a third one thousand, depending on their abilities. Then he left. Right off, the first servant went to work and doubled his master's investment. The second did the same. But the man with the single thousand dug a hole and carefully buried his master's money. "After a long absence, the master of those three servants came back and settled up with them. The one given five thousand dollars showed him how he had doubled his investment. His master commended him: 'Good work! You did your job well. From now on be my partner.'* "The servant with the two thousand showed how he also had doubled his master's investment. His master commended him: 'Good work! You did your job well. From now on be my partner.'* "The servant given one thousand said, 'Master, I know you have high standards and hate careless ways that you demand the best and make no allowances for error. I was afraid I might disappoint you, so I found a good hiding place and secured your money. Here it is, safe and sound down to the last cent.'* "The master was furious. 'That's a terrible way to live! It's criminal to live cautiously like that! If you knew I was after the best, why did you do less than the least? The least you could have done would have been to invest the sum with the bankers, where at least I would have gotten a little interest. 'Take*

the thousand and give it to the one who risked the most. And get rid of this "play-it-safe" who won't go out on a limb. Throw him out into utter darkness. –Matthew 25:14-29 (The Message).'

Taking a risk and faith will advance your career. Specific and thoughtful plans to increase performance and profits can yield success. Taking calculated risks can elevate the performance of global companies, individual professionals, and community-based organizations. People everywhere are assessing their talents and putting them to work in the marketplace. The unknown companies with great talent on staff will put their name and reputation on the line to increase performance, gain public awareness, and increase profitability. These companies calculate the cost and benefit of investing their talent in a specific initiative. Professionals take risks and become entrepreneurs to fully leverage their knowledge and skills. Global brands such as Costco, Google, and Apple have started from the ideas and risk taking of unknown people with talent.

I demonstrated strong mathematical skills in elementary school and set my mind to become a certified public accountant. I did not know a CPA but I read about the profession. In high school, a teacher suggested I divert my aspirations toward bookkeeping because becoming a CPA was difficult. He was right. It was hard, long and expensive but I was willing to make the investment. I finally became a CPA in 1992 and then leveraged that skill set to follow my interests in operations management. I acquired the support and skills necessary to make the transition from finance to operations which utilized my accounting background. Senior leaders at American Express noticed my skills and gave me the opportunities to demonstrate my competency. The result: a career from internal auditor through senior vice president of operations. This parable demonstrates two men taking a risk and investing money for a profit compared to how I took a chance on my skill and passion to achieve my goals. Taking a risk translates into believing the odds are in your favor to receive an incremental reward. If you invest your skills, your value will increase. If you invest in your skills, your return on investment will be increased. If you use your influence, your reputation will be expanded. Do you take the safe and easy solution? Are you willing to risk it all to win?

Taking a calculated risk creates momentum to address the next challenge.

• • •

41 Lead and Follow

"If you want to be perfect, go, sell your possessions and give to the poor, and you will have treasure in heaven. Then come, follow me." When the young man heard this, he went away sad, because he had great wealth. Then Jesus said to his disciples, "Truly I tell you, it is hard for someone who is rich to enter the kingdom of heaven. Again I tell you, it is easier for a camel to go through the eye of a needle than for someone who is rich to enter the kingdom of God." –Matthew 19:21-24 (NIV). A leader who can change direction to become a follower is an example of godliness.

A time comes in every career to alternate between leading and following to achieve goals. Geese fly in a "v" formation and alternate leaders from the flock. The objective of the formation is to leverage the energy of the entire group to create less wind resistance and to have visual assurance regarding who is on the team. As a result of the formation, flying is easier, the distance traveled per minute is increased, and visual communication is possible at all times. A leader can be the person with the title or the informal leader who has the courage and the respect of others. A follower supports the leader (like honking geese in flight) and steps up when the leader needs to step away.

At work, at home. and in the community, we are like the collective church, *"we are all members of one body."* –1 Corinthians 12:7 (NIV).

The ability to lead and follow is centered on attitude. One's attitude is defined by his or her disposition with regard to a person or thing.

The right attitude and humility support interchanging roles—leaders who can be followers and followers who can be leaders. Begin each day by putting aside titles, power plays, and tenure entitlements to work effectively with others to achieve corporate goals or lifetime accomplishments.

The following scenario might exist in your career. Today your dominant skills are project management, requiring you to direct all discussions and actions for the team to get the time, cost, and benefit plan completed for management review. While next month an engineer directs the same group to get the business requirements documented for feasibility and cost finalization. All tasks lead to a weekly update to the executive team of the company. You lead the update to the executive team this week, someone else leads the following week, a third leads four weeks in a row, and another does not lead until next year.

Can you be the highest ranked person in the group but have the attitude of a successful follower? Can you gain the attitude of a confident leader when you are the most junior person on the team? In the final analysis, there is opportunity for all.

For the last two years, I intentionally have positioned myself to assume no titles in my community service work. I simply want to work hard, be engaged, and achieve results. When I am asked to assume the role of chairperson of a committee, I respectfully decline. My goal is to be an informal leader and great follower as is necessary in order for the group to achieve results. I govern myself in the v formation with the ability to lead as well as drop back so someone else can lead.

There is a wealth of knowledge to gain when we humble ourselves to lead or follow, as needed.

• • •

42 Give Back

Remembering the words the Lord Jesus himself said, "It is more blessed to give than to receive." –Acts 20:35 (NIV). Blessings in different forms come to those who give and to those who receive.

Numerous opportunities to give transpire in a career. While ascending the corporate ladder, pausing to help someone else advance his or her career is gratifying. The habit of each person in society giving back by helping another person will improve communities and organizations. Pooling the collective resources of neighbors and colleagues gives us control over outcomes and it feels good.

Give to those who cannot pay it back. It is easy to give to get something in return. However, it is honorable to give and expect nothing in return. Pay it forward with your time, knowledge, and resources. Repay the kindness you have received by being kind to others. A strong community has generations of citizens taking care of each other. Create and perpetuate the circle of giving. Just because you give, does not mean that the receiver will immediately get the expected benefits. Some giving results in a deferred benefit to the receiver. Our job is to keep giving. God will ensure the blessing is received at the right time.

During all levels within my career (staff accountant through senior vice president to entrepreneur), I have offered advice and support to colleagues, friends, and strangers regarding overcoming career obstacles. Many people have cried and cursed in my office about negative feelings regarding the workplace. The issues have ranged from inaccurate assessments of performance, being caught in a layoff, overlooked for a promotion, demeaning treatment from a boss, peer conflict, contributions not being recognized, lack of confidence in the boss, and work–life choices. While I always offer a shoulder to cry on, it is only for a minute or two before we must come up with the game plan. The time I spend with others is my way of giving back so that someone else can avoid or more easily navigate some of the issues I had to suffer through.

One day a young lady came in my office ready to quit and sue because she felt sabotaged. Her claim was that her work was not fairly represented when compared with others given some extenuating shift and staffing differences. We talked about the performance data and how to have a less emotional reaction to her boss's feedback. And if her boss was right, what was she going to do to improve? Was she going to let one person and one bad performance period push her out the door? Finally, we talked about giants—situations that seem larger than life and undefeatable. I told her that giants do fall. She needed to stop crying and complaining, do her job to the best of her ability, and keep track of her progress with her boss. Ironically, her boss left the company a few months later. She worked harder and improved her performance. When she walked out of my office, I thought about how different it would have been for me if I had someone to talk to earlier in my career. Maybe I would have had less bad days. Everyone needs someone to talk to for a reality check, push forward, and support. Are you willing to give someone your time and support to help them reach new levels of success? Are you too busy to help a junior-level person in your company or community?

In the community, I treasure my time teaching children to read, mentoring, tutoring math, and building leadership skills in teenagers (changing attitudes). When I examine my life, I get the greatest joy from what I have learned by giving to others and seeing them succeed.

You do not need permission or a title to give back.

• • •

43 Improve The Culture

Make a tree good and its fruit will be good, or make a tree bad and its fruit will be bad, for a tree is recognized by its fruit. –Matthew 12:33 (NIV). *How good and pleasant it is when God's people live together in unity!* –Psalms 133:1 (NIV). The environment we produce influences results.

People create the culture in the workplace, and the culture is the result of its people. Defining the level of professionalism and competency of a person simply by looking at their organizational title is often inaccurate. Likewise, the day-to-day work environment of a specific company cannot be determined by looking at the logo. Our compatibility with a specific leadership style or company culture greatly varies from person to person. Culture is not written on a glossy 2x3½ card nor is culture determined by shirts, ties, suits, jeans, dresses, and work boots.

Assessing the culture is important if you are an outsider interviewing to join an organization and if you are inside an organization desiring to improve your career. The character qualities of the people in a company will influence the culture of that company. When looking for a job or a leader, assess attributes such as: authenticity, integrity, consistency, generosity, and competitiveness. Conflicting opinions will exist on whether a culture or leader is good or bad. Therefore, ask questions and look around. If you do not work well in an aggressive environment with demanding deadlines and leaders that yell, you might not want to take a job at the Eat What You Kill Company or in the Win At All Cost department. Likewise, the management team should assess if a tense and aggressive workplace is the most productive way to do business. You must observe the intangible aspects of the workplace to determine if you belong there.

Additionally, everyone is responsible for setting and enhancing the culture. It takes one person at a time to improve a culture, and we all have the ability to be a positive influence in a company's culture. That also means understanding the subculture of an organization. The subculture has two dimensions: what people do when management is not looking and what behavior management allows to continue in opposition to the stated culture. Successful organizations have one culture supported by all people in the organization. Alignment with the culture allows people to operate according to the vision, mission, and value messages. Out of sync behaviors create subcultures which undermine organizational effectiveness.

In my career I have had to assess my character and the culture fit of the organization at regular intervals. Fortunately I have had some great bosses and worked for great companies.

I worked in a very analytical organization where people preferred to work autonomously with little interaction with others. I, however, am an extreme extrovert. When I started working in the group and would say hello to colleagues, they would not respond. I discovered it was hard to figure out who was working on what. This lack of interaction meant that we were not leveraging the full power of the intellectual capital and people were not connected. I took on the process of getting people engaged through group lunches, intra-departmental interactions, new employee orientation with colleagues, and a simple process of acknowledging each other. Later, when I became senior vice president, I attended every new hire training class to ensure I met employees within three months of being hired to set the tone for the culture of caring for employees and customers. In those initial meetings, I empowered new employees to be intellectually curious by: asking questions and expecting timely answers, giving them insight into how a positive attitude supported being an extraordinary employee, and relaying the importance of employee fringe benefits to support their career aspirations. These messages on the first day of work set a positive tone linked to a culture that valued employees and their contributions. How do you influence the workplace culture?

As a course of action, routinely ask yourself what you can do to improve the culture. Starting points include opening the lines of communication between colleagues, demonstrating positive character attributes, and working collaboratively toward the company mission.

Effective workplace cultures create harmony between employees, leadership, and customers to increase loyalty and profits.

• • •

44 Prioritize

Ezra had committed himself to studying the Revelation of God, to living it, and to teaching Israel to live its truths and ways. –Ezra 7:10 (The Message). Ezra, a priest, scholar, and expert in matters involving truths and ways of God, had the right priority.

Sequencing tasks provides order and gives priority to one task over another. The tasks can be literal such as a to-do list, to-be-completed lists, development plans, project plans, or bucket lists. The tasks could be symbolic representing family, self, career, education, faith, salvation, and goals. We create a logical order for life and career goals but how do we factor in spiritual priorities?

The Bible gives guideposts for putting matters of eternal life ahead of life on earth. As such, believing in God is foundational to setting priorities. *"Did I not tell you that if you believe, you will see the glory of God?"* –John: 11:40. There is a spiritually guided order for life which puts belief in God and His will first and before everything else. Believing in God as the first priority allows us to live life in the intended order. Our belief system shapes all our thoughts and actions. The lack of a spiritual and moral foundation can result in random thoughts and actions leading to disarray. Depending on God's plan for your life, the order of priorities will differ from person to person. Once the foundation is set, life can begin to make sense. Believing in God does not mean mistakes and struggles will not occur. Given the infinite number of choices available in life a wrong decision is inevitable. Questions arise with no perfect answer. Should you go to college directly after high school or work for two years to earn the money for tuition? Focus exclusively on career and postpone having a family or should you get married, raise a family, and postpone your career?

Conflicts regarding setting priorities happen when one thing is the stated priority but our actions prioritize something else. For example, professionals will say that the family is a high priority and yet come home late every evening leaving limited quality time with the spouse and children. Also, parents say children are a priority but don't go to church as a family, are distracted with work at the dinner table, miss most athletic games, don't read books together, and don't sit down to talk about life. Don't get me wrong, I know having a job and going to work are essential to a family. However, work is not the highest order of life. Out of order and conflicting priorities result in guilt and uneasiness—persistent unsettled thoughts.

My life was out of order. It is commonly called work life balance. I made my career my number one priority—intended and unintended. I loved my job, and I believed in God too. I was blessed to have a job I loved, find a husband, have children, a great home, financial security, trusted friendships, perform community service, and more. God and my family were my stated priorities but I spent more time in the office, on business trips, on my Blackberry, preparing for the next presentation, and coaching employees. I had this lingering guilt about not spending time with my husband and children. I was always edgy. I believed in God, lived like a Christian but something was wrong. I would ask God for the desires of my heart, and it seemed that He always gave them to me. I was happy, but not at peace. On March 4, 2008, I was in New York City making a presentation to the CEO of American Express and his team. The presentation went well and as I was preparing to go back to North Carolina, I got a call that my five-year-old daughter was having a grand mal seizure. I panicked, asked EMS to call my husband, and I ran to the airport. The trip home was delayed by four hours. Sitting in LaGuardia Airport, I had time to think. Reality set in—my life was out of order. I resolved with God that I would change it. I vowed that I would trust Him for all things, quit my job, become a better wife and mother, study the Bible for spiritual growth, and allow Him to direct my life. All I wanted in return was for my daughter to live. We had a deal before I boarded the US Airways jet. I finally got to Greensboro at midnight, and Sophia had been released from the hospital. She was in bed and did not remember anything regarding the seizure or the hospital. My soul was renewed. I kept my end of the deal with God, He kept His, and Sophia has never had another seizure. Today, an indescribable peace exists in my heart and mind. I put my faith in God first and foremost. As a result, I study the Bible and have become a better wife (more work to do), a better mother, a community volunteer, an author, and a joy-filled person. *But in all these things we are completely victorious through God who showed his love for us.* –Romans 8:37 (NCV).

Today is the best day to prioritize to fulfill your aspirations without guilt.

• • •

45 Manage Relationships

Two are better than one, because they have a good return for their work: If one falls down, his friend can help him up. But pity the man who falls and has no one to help him up! –Ecclesiastes 4:9-10 (NIV). God created relationships for the benefit of working together and being a positive influence.

Strong workplace relationships help professionals manage through business protocol, navigate daily agendas to get the job done, and share in the celebration of victories. Healthy workplace relationships are essential for ambitious men and women. The operative word is healthy which is constructive and beneficial to the company.

Key adjectives describe healthy workplace relationships—unbiased, helpful, balanced, trustworthy, respectful, team player, valued, cohesive, influential, mutually beneficial, friendly, inspiring, empowering, instructive, inclusive, compassionate, supportive, and motivating. Is your behavior represented by one of these adjectives? People within the company are responsible for how well employees work together. The reward system for people who foster effective relationships is usually consistent and public, while the consequences for impeding healthy working relationships can be punitive, swift, and direct. Managing relationships is important because winning cultures need the full cooperation of the employee base to meet company goals. New and seasoned professionals within an organization need to depend on colleagues to collectively advance the performance of the entity. A weak or missing link could cause lost revenue and unnecessary expense.

Managing relationships is a skill set to be mastered. A delicate balance is needed to effectively manage relationships to garner ongoing collaboration, cooperation, and shared achievement of goals. Managing relationships employs a spectrum of approaches. Fostering positive relationships and camaraderie is one approach that can be an endless task for management and between peers. Daily colleague interaction will yield a positive or negative outcome. To effectively manage, approach interactions with the attitude of a team player with an honest and stated purpose, be flexible about compromise, be willing to reciprocate, be respectful, and give credit where credit is due. Are you effectively managing relationships with your peers?

Impaired judgment is the common root cause for poor workplace relationships. In my experience three major occurrences can impair judgment and create bad working relationships. First, mixing business and friendship creates an atmosphere of expected favoritism between parties and outsiders begin to distrust the judgment of the observed friends. A special note, when leaders become too familiar with their direct reports, impartiality is lost. Expectations unconscientiously change when friendships manifest at work. Leaders should avoid personal relationships with employees. To maintain a wanted personal friendship, limit directly working together.

Second, holding a grudge against someone at work impairs judgment. The issue could be minor, major, legitimate, documented, and possibly proven. However, letting the issue transition into ineffectively managing relationships makes it detrimental to the parties involved and the company. Let the issue go and proceed or run the risk of failing at work.

Last, would be the influence of bad behavior in the workplace. Sometimes, professionals adopt observed bad behavior and attitudes. The he-does-it-so-why-can't-I syndrome is bad for everyone. The syndrome clouds judgment because bad behavior appears to be accepted and therefore assumed to be appropriate behavior. Using profanity when talking to people or about people at work can destroy working relationships. We rationalize that the boss does it all the time so cursing must be acceptable. The problem is that you are not the boss and using profanity toward a colleague is disrespectful.

In 1983 when I was just five months out of undergraduate school, my boss called me into his office. He told me that I was doing a good job and was becoming well respected. He went on to suggest that I manage relationships in the office to avoid negative influences and bad office politics. He educated me on the perception of being connected to conversations even if I were only listening. *Bad company corrupts good character.* –1 Corinthians 15:33 (NIV). This advice over the last 30 years has been a cornerstone to how I manage professional and personal relationships. As a teenager, my aunt often told me that birds of a feather flock together and one bad apple spoils the whole barrel. I combined the advice to ensure that positive energy was present in my workplace relationships. My relationship agenda is to ensure senior leaders are aware of my contributions, create a work team without conflict, get the job done in partnership with colleagues, break barriers, demonstrate gratitude, and progress to the next project.

Manage relationships through healthy workplace interactions and consistently apply good judgment.

• • •

46 Influence

May the God of hope fill you with all joy and peace as you trust in him, so that you may overflow with hope by the power of the Holy Spirit. –Romans 15:13 (NIV). The influence of the indwelling Holy Spirit brings hope, joy, and peace to empower you to handle people and situations.

Influence can affect, change, sway, inspire, shape, and win over. The source of influence evolves with maturity, exposure, and personal experience. The skill of influence is necessary in business and life. Influence tends to informally start through peer-to-peer interactions to point others toward a desired outcome. Humility and care are important components to effectively give and receive influence. Influence is usually unsolicited and is sometimes unrecognized until after it happens.

To wield influence or accept influence; opportunity, character, and relationships must be presented. Circumstances arise when input and guidance are needed. These opportunities to help are prime places for known influencers who possess an aura of trustworthiness and respect. The aura is magnetic and translates into a connection which encourages influence. Influence is a give and receive. Someone of influence shaped you into a dynamic person which means you have the power to pay it forward by being a positive influence.

The sphere of influence has become borderless. Direct and indirectly, we should seize every moment as an opportunity to be a positive influence in business and life. Most of my influential moments have been spiritually guided, the result of making recommendations, and explaining why. Influence is different from inspiration because of intent. When influencing, I intend to deliver specific information for a specific purpose. Influence aims to get buy-in more often than not. In the office, I do my fact finding, gather my evidence, and put together my talking points in preparation for the discussion, debate, argument, vote, or decision. When tutoring and mentoring, I use generationally relevant material to get children and adults to see the probability of success. Influence is an extraordinary responsibility and makes you accountable for conclusions reached and not reached. The environment to influence can include the boardroom, conference room, classroom, learning center, library, church, coffee shop, dining room table, cell phone conversation, car, playground, sidewalk, and airplane. When I fail to influence and something goes wrong, I feel a sense of responsibility. Do you influence when you should or do you let people figure it out for themselves? Influence can happen with the simple gesture of a smile, mentoring, and making a decision. You do not need to have a leadership position to influence. Influence can happen between any two people.

I attempt to use influence to accomplish my work with others. People are less likely to take responsibility for actions dictated to them. A suggestion from a person people trust is likely to yield the desired action. I asked my colleagues on the executive committee of an organization for support on a first time initiative that required a binding contract and upfront payment of several thousand dollars for a fundraiser. The natural response was questioning related to the rate of return, the risk of failure, and other options. I had done the subcommittee work and knew the plan for the fundraiser was well thought out and would be implemented by a strong group. After much discussion and follow-up, the committee agreed to proceed with the event. Factors supporting the decision included source of the request, track record of success from the subcommittee, importance of the programming, and relationship. The event was a tremendous success. My ability to influence this group in the future was strengthened by positive performance of the event, being responsive to the request for data, and maintaining healthy working relationships.

Influence can nudge people toward new routes to achieve success.

• • •

47 Transform

Do not conform to the pattern of this world, but be transformed by the renewing of your mind. Then you will be able to test and approve what God's will is—his good, pleasing and perfect will. –Romans 12:2 (NIV). Paul wrote a letter to the Roman church about the need for a mindset change still relevant today. Conformity is temporary and superficial. Instead, we need to be renewed by transforming how we think which will direct our actions to fulfill God's plan.

Inside of a career, change is the constant and should be embraced. Transformation means change and evolution. Change can be intentional, unintentional, voluntary, involuntary, expected, and unexpected. In the final analysis, everything is subject to change, and every day there will be something different. The different, is usually better. The common lingo in business for moving performance to a higher level is change, transformational, breakthrough performance, barrier breaking, reengineering, six sigma, lean, lead, market leading, business development, and revolutionary. The people involved in the move to the next level of performance are known as high potential, change agents, change leaders, transformation experts, engineers, account managers, relationship managers, sales and development leaders, and progressive leaders.

Organizations are looking for employees who want to be a part of change and lead change. How do you respond to change? Some of the ways to benefit from the cycles of change include: being innovative, being curious, playing a part in the change design, leading the organization through the change, learning new skills, developing new and expanded workplace relationships, increasing your sphere of influence, making recommendations for improvement, and discovering new interests and passions.

A looming question for those experiencing unexpected change is "What am I going to do?" This question implies confusion and fear. No one will usually answer your question. Unexpected change is better addressed by acknowledging the change impact, stating your continued value, and being specific about your next steps. Replace the question with a statement such as "given the consolidation of companies, my six sigma certification can benefit the combined organization, and I will pursue opportunities in quality control." This statement opens a dialogue in response to your stated plan. Being direct puts you in the driver's seat and says you are taking control of your destiny. In summary, change makes you think differently about where you are and where you are going—standing still is not an option.

Industry consolidations, economic downturns, recessions, reengineering, competitive advantage, margin pressure, in-sourcing, outsourcing, regulatory change, and personal responsibilities are some of the reasons transformation has taken place in my career. The rationale for change caused me to think about the new environment and my continued impact. As a determined and confident professional, I have found new opportunities to add value through each evolution. The changes have included new titles, new responsibilities, new bosses, new location, new salary, and an exit plan. Each change required that I think differently about how to contribute and what was next for me. The outcome of change has been and continues to be beneficial.

I was assigned to a line of business as my primary responsibility and a major scope of my job. About one year into my role, I was advised that the profitability of that business was under question. My job as part of a cross-functional team was to change the product configuration and downsize the operation. It was my first opportunity to transform, reengineer, and change a business. My assignment was to eliminate one product in exchange for another. The data directed the team to which customers would receive an alternate product, who would not receive a product, and how many positions would no longer be needed. We flawlessly implemented the plan. I had reengineered many positions including my own. Most of people in those positions were moved to another product line. Within two years, I was back on a transformation team for my then current product line. Again the product significantly changed, positions were eliminated, and people (including me) were moved to yet another area. Was it bad luck following me or was it a dynamic business model that required constant improvements? What role can you play in transforming your business? Will you make a choice to be part of the transformation?

Transform to signify you are open to the benefits of change.

• • •

48 Inspire

The angel said to me, "These words are trustworthy and true. The Lord, the God who inspires the prophets, sent his angel to show his servants the things that must soon take place. –Revelations 22:6 (NIV). Inspiration guides us to new possibilities.

To inspire and to be inspired benefits all professionals. Inspiration creates a vision beyond current expectations. To be inspired transforms a thought into unbound passion and purpose. Unexpected people can have an inspiring quality. We look up literally and figuratively to be inspired. The upward attention begins with God and trickles down to His servants. Inspiration is possible between people with commonalities—lifestyle, aspirations, obstacles, careers and perspectives. Inspiration can have a simple child-like quality that captures the heart and mind. The captive mind moves into a new realm of possibilities—"I can" and "I will" become the new outlook. We know God makes all things possible, now it is up to us to take inspiration to the next level. A spark from someone can become inspiration in a career.

Effective leaders inspire inside and outside of the company. Inspired employees work effortlessly and inspired consumers spontaneously purchase. These actions lead to profitable business for inspiring leaders.

Inspire through the truth and not tricks and myths. Let the unique and unfiltered passion of your heart remind you and others that we are all great. We are great and not perfect. Inspiration is a natural outgrowth of your personality. Leverage what causes you to connect most with others as your source of inspiration. As your career progresses, the inspiration you project and the inspiration you receive can be topics leaders refer to when discussing your advancement. What inspires you? How do you inspire others?

I inspire through storytelling about my life, career, and spirituality. I allow people to see me at my best and worst. The stories center on the obstacles I have overcome to renew my relationship with God and to gain financial security, my dream job, and family balance. I did not wake up one day with the intent to be inspiring, it just happened without me knowing. Friends and colleagues started to tell me I inspired them. I did not fully understand how; but I was humbled the first time and I remain humble today. My intent is to empower women and men through real examples and stories that break down barriers. These barriers can be differences in educational experience, race, religion, birthright, and title. These erected walls become monuments of fear that keep us from the next level. Life is a gift from God. My life story moves across the continuum from public housing projects, educational priorities, death of my parents, miscarried pregnancies, the corner office, and now author. The Bible, children, and the victories of others inspire me.

In March 2011, the Junior League invited me to be a guest speaker on the subject of "Women in Transition." The presentation centered on why I had given up my executive position and how I embraced my new life. I was candid about the fear and simultaneous joy I felt when I made the decision to leave my career. I expressed that I had no regrets and received daily benefits from the investment I was making in family. The audience was very curious about work life choices. I was honest about my initial feelings of emptiness being without a title in a world where we assess people based on position. I also shared how watching my daughter become a better reader made me cry. The presentation received strong positive feedback. So much so, I was invited to be a speaker in May of that year on the topic of influence. During the May conference, a young lady came up to me to share what an inspiration I had been in March. Due to our discussion on transition, she was inspired to quit her job and come home to be with her family full time. I congratulated her and we hugged as a sign of support and sisterhood. How we impact people to take action is unknown. Are you transparent with your life so that people might learn and be inspired by you?

Inspire so that others can overcome a challenge to achieve their personal best.

• • •

49 Leadership

The God of Israel spoke, the Rock of Israel said to me: 'When one rules over people in righteousness, when he rules in the fear of God, he is like the light of morning at sunrise on a cloudless morning, like the brightness after rain that brings grass from the earth. –2 Samuel 23:3-4 (NIV). Leadership rooted in the love of God provides daily renewal and unencumbered growth.

Open and viral conversations are taking place about admired leadership qualities, leader errors, leadership development programs, accessible leaders, opportunities to become a leader, informal leadership, leadership quotes, leadership models, and taking leadership to the next level. Why is leadership such a hot topic? A company, a community, and a career are doomed without leadership. The notion of strong leadership involves every member of the organization being accountable to drive and deliver performance consistent with the vision and mission. Leadership responsibilities should have a safe landing on the desk of any professional who is aligned with the goals of the company. Leadership qualities are not dependent on assigned titles. Titles bring structure to organizations while it is the people at all levels that bring forth leadership to run the organization. Accordingly, every employee has the potential to be interchangeable with the CEO on a given day or in a given situation. The most relevant leadership is a natural synergy that causes employees to intellectually and emotionally connect their job value to the greater performance targets of the organization. Leadership happens when entry level employees through the executive team address customer requests, train and develop colleagues, fulfill transactions, solve problems, improve processes, and comply with regulations to drive profitability. Additionally, leadership motivates people to complete the job correctly the first time. It always links back to the organization's strategy.

Leadership with a title is an honor with the responsibility of being an example for others to follow. Paul outlines in the Bible the requirements for a godly leader in the church as follows–*If anyone wants to provide leadership in the church, good! But there are preconditions: A leader must be well-thought-of, committed to his wife, cool and collected, accessible, and hospitable. He must know what he's talking about, not be over fond of wine, not pushy but gentle, not thin-skinned, not money-hungry. He must handle his own affairs well, attentive to his own children and having their respect. For if someone is unable to handle his own affairs, how can he take care of God's church? –1 Timothy3:1-6* (The Message). The lesson here hits on two points: the qualities necessary before acceptance into a leader role and the conduct standards for a leader. In other words, the overriding qualities of leadership center on a good reputation, family commitment, composure, approachability, knowledge, discipline, compassion, confidence, financial integrity, and organizational skills. Note, these qualities can be applicable inside or outside the church, whether you have a leadership title or are an individual contributor.

Today, psychological and competency-based tests predict leadership effectiveness. The results do not always identify the right candidates for positions or promotions. A reliable measure for leadership can be found in the demonstrated behavior of a person on the job. I wonder; how many embezzlers have passed a leadership assessment? How would you assess your leadership? What we do in leadership is a reflection of our value system. Leaders overly focused on profitability may implement weak employee benefits. Leaders aspiring to get promoted quickly might prioritize projects with revenue benefits and lower quality before projects that increase expenses form improved quality control. Leaders interested in public recognition may not acknowledge the contribution of the team.

My leadership track record started as a teen by self-governing my behavior and being compassionate. This personal accountability was followed by a formal election into high school student government leadership. Thirty-five years of leadership has been an excellent training ground. My leadership roles have included: peer influence, collaboration on multifunctional teams, brainstorming, entry-level manager positions, idea generation, strategic planning, ownership of a problem that I did not create, various vice president positions, member of board of directors, Sunday School teacher, mother, and mentor. The defining qualities of my leadership include high moral character, reverence for people, and focus on the solution. Projects have failed in my career but rarely have leadership issues surfaced. Bad project results can be chalked up to a lesson learned to improve the next project. On the other hand, leadership errors can have permanent negative implications in the workplace, in the community, and within the family. I strive to make leadership qualities the first thing you see, hear, and read about me.

My leadership motto is to be mutually beneficial. What can I do to improve the business, people, and customers to demonstrate effective leadership? On one occasion, I was appointed to a board of directors and asked to dive in with little orientation. As a member of the finance committee, I committed myself to immediately learn, analyze, praise, share concerns, and provide recommendations to improve performance. Supporting the staff with a vote of confidence while ensuring a sense of urgency sent a message of a partnership to solve the issues. As leaders we can bring water or gas to a situation. Water to put out the fire and bring relief or gas to bring tension and prolong the issue. Are you stepping up to lead in new ways?

Are people benefiting from your leadership? Is the business better because of your leadership?

Leadership reflects what you value.

• • •

50 Connect the Dots

And we know that all things work together for good to them that love God, to them who are the called according to his purpose. –Romans 8:28 (KJV). God has a purpose for the faithful which brings together everything we need for a rich and rewarding life.

The Next Level: Breakthrough Performance Anchored By Faith paints the picture of a greater purpose for our lives. It brings together several important considerations for how a person should perceive him or herself and drive superior performance. *The Next Level* suggests we show up at work with our faith as a reflection of character and talents. The personal satisfaction and peace we receive through spirituality has value beyond our salary, fringe benefits, and title.

In many ways, *The Next Level* combines intelligence quotient (IQ), emotional quotient (EQ), and spiritual quotient (SQ) to offer a balanced perspective on life. Respectively, the three quotients examine logic, compassion, and purpose which are excellent guides for a career. What role are you willing to let faith play in your career? Can your performance use a boost by mastering the fundamentals? Are you ready to incorporate accelerator performance tactics into your workday? Are you capable of a breakthrough contribution?

Connect the dots between who you are and the skills you possess. Be intentional about how your performance is influenced by your faith. God will support you if you ask Him.

Use the following notes pages to document the character attributes (Chapters 1-25) and performance tactics (Chapters 26 -49) that are significant for you to make your faith a part of your plan to progress in life, the community, and at work. Your breakthrough is coming.

Connecting the dots between faith, skills, and purpose will catapult you toward outstanding performance.

• • •

Notes

Notes

Notes

Notes

Notes

Notes

AFTERWORD

God makes available to mankind the opportunity to achieve immeasurable success at work, in the community, and at home. *The Next Level* points you in the direction to examine your behavior and performance to ascend to new heights. If you have questions about God or want to personally develop a relationship with the God I refer to in *The Next Level,* the Bible is specific about what you should do. *The word of faith we are proclaiming: That if you confess with your mouth, "Jesus is Lord," and believe in your heart that God raised him from the dead, you will be saved. For it is with your heart that you believe and are justified, and it is with your mouth that you confess and are saved. As the Scripture says, "Anyone who trusts in him will never be put to shame. For there is no difference between Jew and Gentile—the same Lord is Lord of all and richly blesses all who call on him, for, "Everyone who calls on the name of the Lord will be saved." –*Romans 10:8-13 (NIV).

ABOUT THE AUTHOR

Michelle Gethers-Clark has 29 years of experience as an entrepreneur, executive for American Express Company, and member of several non-profit Boards of Directors. She has blended corporate and community leadership to consult for clients and present lectures to audiences on topics related to character, service, and leadership. Michelle's corporate and personal experiences have been featured in BIZlife, Black Enterprise, and Working Mother magazines. Michelle lives with her husband and two children in Greensboro, North Carolina.

Blog: MICHELLE-THENEXTLEVEL.BLOGSPOT.COM

Twitter: THENEXTLEVEL50

Facebook: THE NEXT LEVEL